Dissent and Protest

DAVID T. NAYLOR

Social Studies Teacher
Cranford High School, Cranford, New Jersey

HAYDEN BOOK COMPANY, INC.
Rochelle Park, New Jersey

To my wife, Mary,
from whom I received much strength
and encouragement
and little dissent and protest.

74281

Library of Congress Cataloging in Publication Data

Naylor, David, 1941—
  Dissent and protest.

  (Hayden American values series)
  SUMMARY: Discusses the causes for past and
present dissent in America and the varying responses
to it by public and private figures.
  Bibliography: p.
  1. Civil rights—United States. 2. Demonstrations
—United States. 3. Dissenters—United States.
4. United States—Social conditions—1945-
[1. Civil Rights. 2. Demonstrations. 3. Dissenters.
4. United States—Social conditions—1945-   ]
I. Title.
JC599.U5N36   309.1'73   73-17106
ISBN 0-8104-5904-3

Printed in the United States of America

      1 2 3 4 5 6 7 8 9   PRINTING

   74 75 76 77 78 79 80 81 82   YEAR

Design A. Victor Schwarz
Editorial S. W. Cook
Production Helen L. Garfinkle
Consultant Dr. Abraham Resnick

Editor's Introduction

How old will you be in the year 2000?

How will the world be different?

If you could choose, what things would you change between now and then?

What would you want to leave unchanged?

Social problems such as discrimination, pollution, crime, and poverty are the result of decisions made in the past. Are there solutions for these and other problems? Will they have changed by the year 2000?

What new challenges are likely to develop?

What choices are now available?

America shares a dominant value with many parts of the world—the idea of a democratic society based on human rights and social justice. This is not always achieved, and there are many disputes over how it can be achieved, but basic documents like the Declaration of Independence and the Constitution express the strong belief that this value is worth the struggle against repression, ignorance, and intolerance. A democratic society depends upon thoughtful and enlightened citizens. The challenges of social issues demand critical inquiry. The choices involve consequences for the future.

The HAYDEN AMERICAN VALUES SERIES: CHALLENGES AND CHOICES presents social issues in contemporary society. This book provides a framework for examining one of these issues. A similar format is found in each book. Each includes:

- Case studies illustrating the issue by focusing on human situations.
- Factual information about the issue which can be used as evidence in making social decisions.
- Divergent views and opposing value judgments showing a variety of values involved in solving the issue.
- Futuristic scenarios illustrating possible consequences of social decisions in future human situations.
- Suggestions for involvement in the issues and the decisions.
- Recommendations for further study.

J. N.

Contents

Dissent
and Protest

Chapter 1

Situations

Her Feet Were Tired

MONTGOMERY, ALA., December 2, 1955—Yesterday a Negro seamstress, Mrs. Rosa Parks, was arrested on her way home from work for failure to comply with a city ordinance regulating seating practices on public buses. Having boarded the Cleveland Avenue bus which she normally takes to return to her home, Mrs. Parks sat in the first row of the section designated for Negro passengers. As more people began to get on the bus with subsequent stops, the "white" section filled up. As provided by city ordinance, the bus driver then asked Mrs. Parks and three other Negro passengers to surrender their seats and permit white passengers to sit in those seats. The three other Negro passengers complied with the bus driver's request, but Mrs. Parks refused. Interviewed later, Mrs. Parks indicated that her refusal was based on the fact that with all of the other seats occupied, she would have had to stand. Since she had worked all day and her feet were tired, she did not wish to stand and thus refused to surrender her seat. Her refusal to move was in violation of the Montgomery city ordinance and was responsible for her arrest.

MONTGOMERY, ALA., December 6, 1955—The arrest of Mrs. Rosa Parks last week for failure to comply with a city ordinance regulating seating on public buses has triggered a significant amount of reaction among Montgomery's Negro citizens. Local Negro leaders, including the Reverend Martin Luther

King, Jr., and the Reverend Ralph Abernathy, have reacted to the arrest and have decided that some form of protest is necessary. Some forty or fifty leaders of various groups within the Negro community met Friday evening, December 2, and apparently decided that, despite the existence of a city ordinance banning boycotts, a boycott of city buses would be an effective means of protesting the arrest of Mrs. Parks since the great majority of bus riders in the city are Negroes.

⸺ Apparently the result of the meeting last Friday evening, a call for a city-wide mass meeting was made. Last night that meeting was held at the Dexter Avenue Baptist Church. The church was packed, as hundreds more gathered outside listening to the main speech delivered by Reverend King. In a speech often interrupted by applause and shouts of approval, Reverend King reviewed the past experiences of Negroes on city buses and called for a city-wide boycott of the buses until Negro citizens received more equitable treatment. "But there comes a time when people get tired," he said. "We are here this evening to say to those who have mistreated us so long that we are tired—tired of being segregated and humiliated; tired of being kicked about by the brutal feet of oppression. We have no alternative but to protest." He stated, "One of the great glories of democracy is the right to protest for right," and added, "Our method will be that of persuasion, not coercion. We will only say to the people, 'Let your conscience be your guide.' "⸺

⸺Following his speech, Reverend King proposed a three-part resolution calling for: (1) courteous treatment by bus drivers; (2) employment of Negro bus drivers on predominantly Negro routes; and (3) seating on a first-come, first-served basis with whites sitting from the front toward the back and Negroes sitting from the back toward the front. Both the resolution and boycott proposals were passed enthusiastically. ⸺

MONTGOMERY, ALA., December 21, 1956—Today, after 381 days during which Montgomery city buses remained virtually empty, the boycott of city buses by Montgomery's Negro citizens came to an end. In the wake of a United States Supreme Court decision invalidating the city's bus segregation ordinance, bus company officials finally capitulated. Thus, for the first time in over a year, Negro passengers again ride city buses.

Although the local chapter of the NAACP did not support the boycott because the three-part resolution did not call for an end of segregated seating, virtually all of Montgomery's Negro citizens refused to ride the buses and either walked to work or used car pools. The boycott began on December 5, 1955, in protest of the arrest of a Negro seamstress, Mrs. Rosa Parks, who refused to surrender her seat. Following a city-wide meeting that night led by Reverend Martin Luther King, Jr., well over ninety percent of the Negroes who normally rode the buses refused to ride them. Thus, the normal daily load of approximately 30,000 to 35,000 Negro passengers was reduced to perhaps 300 to 500 passengers a day.

City officials had tried to break the boycott by arresting and imprisoning boycott leaders, but the city buses remained virtually empty for 381 days. While continuing their direct action of boycotting, the protesters brought suit in Federal District Court challenging the constitutionality of state and local laws requiring segregation on the buses. On November 13, 1956, the Supreme Court of the United States ruled that such bus segregation violated the United States Constitution and ordered the practice stopped, an order which officially went into effect today.

With the long boycott over, hundreds of Negroes met last night in a mass meeting to celebrate their victory. This morning they calmly boarded the buses and sat wherever they chose. Bus segregation in Montgomery, as well as the boycott, is now history.

Letters to the Editor

Gentlemen:

Despite a city ordinance prohibiting boycotts, the Negro inhabitants of Montgomery deliberately flaunted the law. Their disgraceful behavior caused economic hardship and brought shame to the city of Montgomery. Yet, incredibly, the Supreme Court has sided with these lawbreakers. By some form of inexplicable logic, those who have illegally acted have been vindicated while those who have attempted to enforce the law have been rebuked.

Let us make no mistake about the significance of this situation. The Court is saying that good citizens may be successfully coerced by a disgruntled minority. Such a precedent runs contrary to civilized society and no less than societal survival is at stake. This situation is but the initial hole in the dyke. The flood waters of lawlessness and disrespect have now started to spurt through the opening created by the Court. This hole must be plugged and plugged immediately or we will all be swallowed up in a sea of anarchy.

Birmingham, Ala.   Hall Witherington, Ph.D.

Dear Sirs:

The success in Montgomery was due to the patience and restraint of the protesters. Despite severe hardships in some cases, they chose to form car pools or walk to work rather than use city buses. Arrest and intimidation failed to dissuade them and success has failed to corrupt them. This is evidenced by the pamphlet issued shortly after the Court decision which urged the protesters to prove themselves worthy, to be courteous and to behave properly. This is what we must never forget. The true test is when, having challenged a situation and succeeded in changing the practice, the protesters prove themselves worthy of exercising their newly won rights and responsibilities.

Exeter, Mississippi   Philip Johnstone

Dear Sir:

The leftist NAACP has done it again! This communist-oriented group has long sought to destroy the very nature of American society. No longer content with reliance on their commie-symp stooges who sit on the bench in some of our courts, they have entered a new phase with new tactics: economic blackmail and civil disobedience.

Do they really expect us to believe that Rosa Parks acted on her own, that she wasn't put up to this? Do they really believe that we Americans are so blind that we would think the boycott was a "spontaneous reaction" rather than a carefully drawn plan?

We are on to this plot to destroy the America we all love. We know that outside agitators are to blame for what occurred in Montgomery, filling our Negro citizens with lies and fake promises. We know this and will not sit idly by while activities such as these continue. Now is the time for all true Americans to realize the truth about Montgomery. Let's not mistake what happened here.

Montgomery, Alabama   James R. Lee

Sirs:

The Rubicon has been crossed; the first significant step has been taken. All true Americans should rejoice at the recent Supreme Court decision making the practice of maintaining segregation illegal. It has taken this country 180 years but finally we begin to make real for our Negro citizens the ideals on which this country was founded.

But this is only the beginning; many more victories must be won. Montgomery demonstrates what can be done when a people are determined to fight injustice. Negroes throughout this country must rise against similar injustices and good white people must support Negroes in their quest for equality and justice. Unjust laws must be challenged wherever they exist.

Montgomery's Negro community has been charged with violating the law by committing the "illegal" act of boycotting city buses. Isn't it an individual's right to decide whether or not to use public transportation? Isn't it a citizen's right to refuse to support an unjust practice? If a law is immoral or unconstitutional, why should a citizen have to obey it?

The Supreme Court ruled that Montgomery's Negro citizens were "guilty" only of being good citizens by using their constitutional rights to disobey what was clearly an unconstitutional practice. Montgomery's Negro community used their rights with restraint, courage, and conviction. Their goal was just, their means appropriate, their victory deserved.

Chicago, Illinois   David Benjamin

"Good Evening, My Fellow Americans"

"Good evening, my fellow Americans." These now familiar greetings signaled another prime-time television address to the American people by President Richard Nixon. In this April 31, 1970, address, delivered less than two weeks after one announcing an American troop withdrawal from Vietnam of 150,000 troops, President Nixon revealed a new policy decision.

>   To protect our men who are in Vietnam, and to guaran-
> tee the continued success of our withdrawal and Vietnami-
> zation program, I have concluded that the time has come
> for action. . . . In cooperation with the armed forces of
> South Vietnam, attacks are being launched this week to
> clean out major enemy sanctuaries on the Cambodian-Viet-
> nam border. . . . This is not an invasion of Cambodia. . . . We
> take this action not for the purpose of expanding the war
> into Cambodia but for the purpose of ending the war in
> Vietnam, and winning the just peace we all desire.

Clearly anticipating sharp reaction to this decision, President Nixon added:

>   No one is more aware than I of the political conse-
> quences of the action I've taken. . . . I would rather be a
> one-term President and do what I believe was right than to
> be a two-term President at the cost of seeing America be-
> come a second-rate power and see this nation accept the
> first defeat in its proud 190-year history.

Such expectations were not without foundation, for major
protests soon erupted on the campuses of many of the nation's
colleges and universities. On May 1, the day immediately following the President's announcement, Kent State students held
rallies to protest the Cambodian invasion. What began as peaceful protest at this university of 20,000 students degenerated into
more violent acts that evening as several hundred students
marched through downtown Kent, broke windows, set trash cans
afire, and damaged cars along their route.

The next day protesters gathered but it was not until evening that violence reappeared. This time students burned the
one-story wooden ROTC building on campus. When firemen attempted to put out the blaze, students threw stones at them and
cut their fire hoses. Such actions prompted Kent's mayor to
appeal to the Governor of Ohio for immediate assistance. In-
censed at these incidents, Governor Rhodes vowed, "If these
anarchists get away with it here, no campus in the country is
safe. . . . We are going to eradicate the problem. . . ." He immediately dispatched National Guardsmen to the campus. They arrived within an hour and helped restore order by midnight.

Governor Rhodes personally visited Kent on May 3, declared
martial law, and banned all future demonstrations on the Kent
State campus. Despite these measures and the presence of

some 600 National Guardsmen on campus, further incidents broke out that evening which ended when Guardsmen used tear gas to chase students into dormitories.

On Monday, May 4, a major confrontation developed between the students and the Guardsmen. Despite the ban on demonstrations, several hundred students gathered at noon near the burned ROTC building and asserted their right to assemble peacefully. Students going to lunch and to classes swelled the number in the area. When the Guardsmen attempted to have the crowd disperse, the students refused. Bedecked with helmets and gas masks, the Guardsmen fired tear gas into the midst of the students, who taunted them with verbal epithets and hurled rocks and debris at the Guardsmen. The use of the tear gas was somewhat successful in getting the students to move and the crowd broke into groups. A contingent of Guardsmen moved over a hill away from the Commons toward a parking lot in pursuit of one group of students. They then moved back up the hill to disperse other groups of students. Buoyed by what appeared to be a retreat by the Guardsmen, the students who had been chased to the parking lot began to follow the retreating Guardsmen. At the crest of the hill the Guardsmen stopped and turned around. A series of staccato noises filled the air, followed by cries of horror and disbelief. The Guardsmen had fired over thirty rounds of live ammunition. Four students lay dead and ten others were wounded, three seriously, including one permanently paralyzed by a spinal wound. None of the four dead students—two girls and two boys—was described as a revolutionary or hardcore radical.

Conflicting interpretations of the pattern and circumstances of these events abounded. Although officials of the National Guard asserted that the troops had been fired upon by a sniper, no evidence of sniper activity was uncovered. No criminal action was brought by officials against any of the Guardsmen. Although 24 students and one faculty member were subsequently indicted for their activities during the several days, very few convictions resulted. A Gallup poll shortly after the shootings revealed that a majority of Americans (58 percent) felt that demonstrating students were primarily responsible for the deaths of the four students. Only a small minority of Americans (11 percent) assigned responsibility for the deaths to the National Guard. What had begun as student protest to a new policy in Indochina tragically brought a new dimension to dissent on the nation's college campuses.

Letters to the Editor

Dear Sir:

Senator Harold Hughes, Democrat of Iowa, clearly assessed the meaning of the Kent State tragedy in his remarks on the Senate floor on May 5th. All Americans should seriously reflect on his words:

> There is no confusion about the fact that this tragedy was a product of the war, just as surely as deaths in combat.
> No responsible person condones violence. No responsible person should condone unwarranted counterviolence.
> The President said that the shooting should "remind us once again that when dissent turns to violence it invites tragedy."
> The corollary of this is that when you equate all dissent with violent insurrection—to the extent of shooting indiscriminately into a crowd of rock-throwing, otherwise unarmed students—you open wounds in the society that are almost beyond healing. . . .

Washington, D.C.   Todd Vernon

Dear Sir:

What hypocrisy, what folly to claim as some that student action on the Kent State campus was justifiable because of Cambodia. Let's call these actions by their right names—arson, riot, assault, and anarchy. We have laws to safeguard ourselves from such acts. We have a right to demand the enforcement of these laws. No civilized people can tolerate such acts.

We must not let ourselves be blackmailed by violence and terrorism. Let's not forget that it was the students who terrorized the town, it was the students who burned down the ROTC building, it was the students who assembled illegally, it was the students who provoked the National Guard with their rocks and taunts. They are the ones who initiated the violence.

The blame must be put squarely where it belongs. It is not President Nixon who is responsible, it is not the National Guard who is responsible, but it is the students themselves who are responsible for the violence on the Kent State campus. They must learn that violence only produces counter-violence. Violent dissent produces anarchy. It can not, it *must* not be tolerated.

Kalamazoo, Michigan   John Michaels

Dear Sir:

This should remind us all once again that when dissent turns to violence it invites tragedy. It is my hope that this tragic and unfortunate incident will strengthen the determination of all the nation's campuses, administrators, faculty and students alike to stand firmly for the right which exists in this country of peaceful dissent and just as strongly against the resort to violence as a means of such expression.

These were the words of President Richard Milhous Nixon upon hearing of the Kent State atrocity. They serve as a classic illustration of what's wrong with this country. Not one word about the inflammatory rhetoric of Governor Rhodes; not one word about the use of *live* ammunition on a university campus; not one word about the fact that two of the four dead students were not even taking part in the demonstration.

There is not even a hint that the authorities must be held responsible for the murder of the four students. No, not one hint, for in President Nixon's eyes, only the students—"bums" he recently called them—were responsible. Such myopia is incredible! When will we admit to the hypocrisy and idiocy of our Vietnam policy, of the prevalence of our racism, of our war against dissent and the young? When will we, as Pogo, admit, "We have met the enemy and the enemy is us"? If Kent State doesn't do it, what in God's name will?

New Brunswick, New Jersey   Helen Miller

Dear Sir:

I could not help but be impressed by the following words of Senator William Saxbe, Republican of Ohio. Far more eloquent that I could ever be, Senator Saxbe clearly points to the crux of the Kent State controversy. I include them for your perusal.

Dr. [Benjamin] Spock said today . . . that this incident shows that our Government would kill rather than allow dissent. That is exactly the way it came over—that this incident shows that our Government would kill rather than permit dissent.

If there is anything that is completely wrong, it is a statement like that, because here are National Guardsmen, scared to death, with no orders to shoot anybody—in fact, I know that they have been impressed at every step of the way, "This is never done except when you are in danger yourself."

But suppose . . . that they are given no ammunition, and they are sent out there, and everyone knows they have no ammunition, and the next thing their helmet is knocked off, their gun is taken away from them, they are publicly humiliated and defenseless.

I wish that we could send our policemen out without guns. I wish we could send all our peace officers out without any means of violence, even a club. But this cannot happen, and today we must be realistic.

Unless this type of disorder is stopped, we are going to have to close our universities. . . .

Laramie, Wyoming   Glenn Raymond

Chapter 2

An Historical Perspective

Stop the Bombing
America: Love It or Leave It
Boycott Lettuce
Remember Wounded Knee
I Have a Dream—One America
Power to the People
Legalize Pot
End Male Chauvinism Now
Keep America Green
Equal Rights for All
End Abortion: Save a Life Today

These slogans are part of the rhetoric of dissent and protest in contemporary America. They are familiar to all of us, for we can scarcely pick up a newspaper or magazine or turn on a radio or television set without being exposed to them.

Groups such as the Black Panthers, the Yippies, the Zippies, the Ku Klux Klan, the Southern Christian Leadership Conference, the National Organization for Women, the Welfare Rights Organization, the Gay Liberationists, the Women's Strike for Peace, the John Birch Society, the Redstockings, the Revolutionary Youth Movement, the Vietnam Veterans Against the War, the People's Party, the American Party, the Congress of Racial Equality, the Socialist Workers Party, the Young Lords, the American Communist Party, the Right to Life, the Young Americans for Freedom, the Christian Anti-Communist Crusade, etc., are in the forefront of the news as they seek to move society in the direction they see as most preferable.

11

Letter writing, sit-in, lie-in, march, picket, boycott, petition, moratorium, confrontation, riot, revolution, bust, preventive detention—these words are an integral part of our contemporary vocabulary. The words are descriptive of the means used by various groups to secure their ends.

Since the mid-1950s, literally hundreds of local, regional, and national groups have formed seeking to change the society of which they are a part. From individual to group concerns, from local to national concerns, from singular, clear targets such as the Vietnam war to multifaceted, nebulous ones such as "The Establishment," from legal means to extralegal means, from nonviolence to violence, from optimism to despair, from constructive alternatives to virtual nihilism, the outpouring of mass dissent and protest is in evidence in contemporary America. America is in a very real sense caught up in change and the demands for change.

Table 2.1 offers support for these assertions. While not all-inclusive, Table 2.1 points to a number of the major demonstrations that occurred in Washington, D.C., between October 1967 and August 1970.

It should be remembered that Washington is but one city within the United States. Granted, its unique status, that of housing the major decision-making forces of the United States government, makes that city a special target of protest activities. Yet on a number of occasions parallel demonstrations of great intensity have occurred simultaneously in other cities and towns throughout the country. And, more frequently, major demonstrations independent of those occurring in the nation's capital have taken place in cities and towns, on college and university campuses, and even on United States military bases across the breadth of this country.

Americans are constantly reminded and informed of the level of dissent and protest activities occurring within the United States by the mass media, the extent and variety of which are unparalleled in the history of mankind. A staff report to the National Commission on the Causes and Prevention of Violence, entitled *Mass Media and Violence*, provides statistics that reveal both the great variety and the extent of the mass media in the United States today. This 1969 report indicated that there are more than 1,700 daily newspapers, more than 570 Sunday newspapers, and more than 8,000 weekly newspapers. There are approximately 650 magazines, more than 2,300 business and trade publications, and countless school, labor-union, and other special publications representing highly specialized interests. In addition, there are approximately 830 television stations, of which 167 are considered educational stations, and almost 6,500 radio stations, of which 355 are educational or public-service stations. Furthermore, the report notes the existence of more than 1,000 publishing houses which produce in excess of 200,000,000 textbooks and 88,000,000 trade books a year. And there are over 10,000 motion-picture theaters and 3,500 drive-in theaters that exhibit the nearly 200 feature films produced annually in the United States as well as feature films from abroad. It should also be recognized that these statistics do not include the total communications resources used by advertisers, who invest some $6 billion in other forms of mass media, including posters, direct-mail, and other forms of display and sales promotion.

While statistics with respect to the great variety of mass media in the United States are impressive, equally if not more important are statistics with respect to the use of mass-media facilities. The report, *Mass Media and Violence*, revealed that 95 percent of American homes have at least one television set and 99 percent have at least one radio. Of American adults 95 percent read a newspaper at least once a week and 90 percent read at least one magazine a month. Approximately 13 percent see a movie during an average week and 33 percent see at least one film a month. On an average day in an average week, 82 percent of the adults watch television for more than two hours, 66 percent listen to the radio for more than one hour, 78 percent read a newspaper (and nearly half of these read both a morning and evening paper), and 37 percent read at least one magazine.

The increasing frequency of dissent and protest activities such as sit-ins, marches, picketing, and holding of large rallies during the late 1960s and early 1970s has generated considerable public and government concern over the news media's— and particularly television's—coverage of these events. Some charge that such activities are actually staged for the television networks. Others suggest that the mere presence of television cameras stimulates protest activities, frequently leading to violence. And still others claim that television distorts the events that do occur, blowing them up far out of proportion to their actual importance.

Charges such as these have emanated from a wide variety of sources, ranging from labor union "hard-hats" to the Vice

Table 2.1. Major Demonstrations Held in Washington, D.C., October 1967 to August 1970

Date	Reason for Protest	Nature of Protest	Sponsor	Size	Violence?
10/21/67	Anti-war	March on the Pentagon	Mobilization Committee To End the War in Vietnam	5,000	Yes
1/21/68	Anti-war	Women's march to the Capitol	The Jeannette Rankin Brigade	3,500	No
2/6/68	Anti-war	Silent prayers for the war dead in Vietnam	Clergy & Laymen Concerned about Vietnam	2,500	No
11/5/68	Lack of choice in '68 Pres. election	March	Students for a Democratic Society (SDS)	800	Yes
1/20/69	Inaugural Parade for Pres. Nixon	Anti-war	Nat. Mobilization Committee To End the War in Vietnam	x	x
1/20/69	Inaugural Parade	Counter-Inaugural movement	SDS and Co-Aim	400	Yes
3/26/69	Anti-war	Women's march from White House to Capitol	Women's Strike for Peace	1,000 to 1,300	No
5/5/69	Anti-war	Pickets in 24-hour vigil before White House	American Friends Service Committee	1,500	No
10/15/69	Anti-war	Candlelight march around White House and rally	D.C. Moratorium Committee	2,000	No
11/11/69	Pro-Vietnam policy	Veterans' Day rally at the Washington Monument	No specific organization	7,000 to 10,000	No
11/13–15/69	Anti-war	March and various demonstrations	New Mobilization Committee To End the War in Vietnam	250,000 to 300,000	Yes

Date	Cause	Activity	Organization	Number	Arrests
2/15/70	Anti-war	Rally and march to the White House	Vietnam Moratorium Committee	400	No
2/19/70	Convictions in Chicago 7 trial	Rally at Watergate Apts.	No specific organization	500 to 600	Yes
4/5/70	Pro-Vietnam policy	Rally and march	Rev. Carl McIntire	10,000 to 15,000	No
4/15/70	Anti-war and Anti-taxes	Rally and picketing	Vietnam Moratorium Committee	2,000	No
5/6/70	Anti-war	Rally	American University students	1,000	Yes
5/9/70	Anti-war	Rally and demonstrations	New Mobilization Committee To End the War in Vietnam	60,000 to 100,000	Yes
5/11/70	Anti-war	Demonstrations; meetings with Congressmen	No specific organization —students	2,000	No
7/4/70	Honor America Day	Rally at Washington Monument	Citizens' committee headed by Bob Hope and the Rev. Dr. Billy Graham	350,000	Yes
8/26/70	Women's Liberation	Rally	Federally Employed Women	x	No

Source: Data compiled by the Library of Congress, Legislative Reference Service, Washington, D.C., and the *New York Times*.

President of the United States. Whether such charges are with or without substance remains in question. What is clear is the role that the mass media has played and continues to play in bringing knowledge of dissent and protest activities to the attention of the American public.

The Task Force on Mass Media and Violence points to the difficulties confronting dissident groups. Most important of these is the educational function, making Americans aware that a problem exists and then urging the corrective steps to be taken. It is this area in which the mass media—particularly television —make their most important contributions.

Broad-based coverage by the white-controlled media of the plight, interests, and needs of black Americans was negligible in the early 1950s. Even following the Supreme Court decision of *Brown v. Board of Education* in 1954, the decision that voided the "separate but equal" doctrine, little attention was given within the white community to the impact of that decision. And the Montgomery bus boycott which began in December 1955 was virtually ignored by the mass media at the time. It was not until the success of that incident, followed by the sit-ins, freedom rides, picketings, and parades, that white America became conscious of the plight of America's black citizens. The Task Force noted:

> These events were unusual, they represented conflict, they had a potentially wide impact, there was action, and the response of the official and nonofficial white South sometimes provided violence. In short, these reactions fitted almost any reporter's definition of "news." Most important, they provided material uniquely suited to the new medium, television.
>
> If only the leaders such as Dr. King had simply called a press conference, briefed the reporters present, and instructed them to go out and report on the deplorable state of race relations in America! If they had, of course, very few, if any, of the white media would have written the story; in many instances, they could not because they did not know how. Even if they had, few people in the white community would have read it. And if whites had read it, few would have perceived the urgency of the situation. Some still don't. The Negro community not only had to get the attention of the white media, they also had to get the attention of the white audience.

The campaign of sit-ins, parades, and picketing at least provided some news coverage of black problems. White Americans, for the first time, were learning that blacks existed as humans, not chattels, and were unhappy about something. Whites also learned that the Negro proposed to do something about his discontent. . . . The television media, presented with action, brought the human aspect of the story to the American home with unprecedented impact and directness.

At one time, a demonstration, a boycott, a sit-in, or any other form of confrontation, even when non-violent, almost guaranteed coverage by news media. Today, the greater number of non-violent demonstrations have reduced their efficacy as a technique for access, but still appeal to traditional news values and provide the action desired by television.

Apparent to any observer of the American scene for the past fifteen years is that this technique for gaining access is used by those who have not been admitted through traditional channels. General Motors, the President of the United States, or the Chamber of Commerce do not need a parade or physical confrontation to attract media attention. Dissenters have the problem of attracting not only media attention, but also public attention. The non-violent confrontation is a press conference for those who cannot otherwise command the attention of the media and its public.

The Roots of Dissent

The attention given to such dissent and protest activities by the mass media often creates the impression that what is happening in recent years is new to America. Nothing could be further from the truth, for even a casual, and most certainly a careful, reading of American history reveals that dissent and protest have deep roots in this country. In a very real sense, America might be regarded as the land of dissent, for it was founded for the most part by dissenters, and dissent and protest have played major roles in shaping the face of contemporary America.

The first permanent English settlement in America was established at Plymouth in 1620, founded by a group of Puritan dissenters who sought to escape from what they regarded as religious oppression in Stuart England. Thus they came to America, where they ultimately succeeded in establishing their own Church. A number of other colonists who came to America in the seventeenth century were likewise religiously motivated, including such groups as the Quakers, the Huguenots, and the Mennonites. The seventeenth century was an era of religious and political dissent, an era when the outcasts, malcontents, and rebels sought outlets in the "new world" denied to them in the old.

Yet for some the colonies did not provide the haven hoped for. Curiously enough, the Puritans, who had left England because of their own dissenting views, refused to tolerate dissent in their colonies, insisting instead upon strict theological orthodoxy. But despite efforts by such groups as the Puritans to establish theocratic government characterized by religious intolerance, dissent was not quelled. Rhode Island and Pennsylvania openly proclaimed religious toleration and thereby attracted various groups of religious dissenters.

Religious dissent was not, however, the only type of dissent prevalent in colonial America. The seventeenth and eighteenth centuries were periods of increased dissent and protest activities, centering primarily on social, economic, and political issues. Taxes, rents, and Indian-colonist relations often served as focal points, sometimes ending in riots and rebellions such as Bacon's Rebellion (1676), the Paxton Boys' uprising (1763), and Shay's Rebellion (1787).

Relations between the colonies and Great Britain were the chief cause of dissent and protest in the eighteenth century. Men such as Patrick Henry, Thomas Paine, Samuel Adams, and Thomas Jefferson stand tall in this context, and such events as the Boston Massacre (1770) and the Boston Tea Party (1773) typify accelerating dissent and protest activities. With the proclamation of the Declaration of Independence in 1776, the colonies embarked on a new path which led to the ultimate adoption of the Constitution in 1788 and the Bill of Rights in 1791.

This new country, created in the midst of revolution, implemented a rather bold and experimental form of government which, if not in actual practice, at least in theory rested upon the "consent of the governed." Although the Bill of Rights was not originally a part of the Constitution, a strong effort was waged to include it. While that effort was not successful in making a Bill of Rights part of the original Constitution, it led to the inclusion of these rights by 1791. It should be remembered that not all of the thirteen colonies originally ratified the Constitution, for North Carolina did not do so until November 1789, and Rhode Island did not do so until May 1790. And of the eleven colonies that did approve the Constitution, three of them —Virginia, Massachusetts, and New York—did so in the apparent belief that a Bill of Rights would be added soon after its adoption. The colonists had had experience with arbitrary government; a Bill of Rights was considered necessary to prevent this new government from developing similar tendencies.

Thus the Bill of Rights added in 1791 provides for individual liberties and guarantees against arbitrary actions by the government against individual citizens. The First Amendment contains the essence of dissent:

> Congress shall make no law respecting an establishment of religion, or prohibiting the free exercise thereof; or abridging the freedom of speech, or of the press, or the right of the people to assemble, and to petition the Government for a redress of grievances.

The United States did not remain a static society, as a comparison of the America of the 1970s with the America of the 1790s quickly reveals. Given an experimental form of government with the philosophic idealism of the Declaration of Independence and the guarantees provided by the Bill of Rights, the United States has been engaged in a process of continual transformation with much of the impetus coming from dissenters, those individuals who have sought to move the country in directions they thought would best approximate the hopes and dreams of the country's citizenry.

The 1830s and 1840s were decades that witnessed a great outpouring of dissent, decades that in a number of ways appear remarkably similar to the 1960s and 1970s. Consider the following reformist concerns during those decades:

- an abolitionist movement greatly concerned with the plight of blacks in America;
- a feminist movement proclaiming equality between the sexes;
- a peace movement, including opposition to the controversial Mexican War;

- a communitarian or alternative-life-style movement which witnessed the founding of almost two hundred groups with from 15 to 900 members each;
- a temperance movement attacking alcohol, the drug considered to be the great evil of its day;
- a health-food movement, a leading spokesman of which was Dr. Sylvester Graham of "Graham cracker" fame;
- a free-public-education movement, though focused at that time on state-supported primary education;
- other causes including prison reform and mental health reform.

After the divisive and costly Civil War, the effects of industrialism were seriously felt. Confronted with major changes in social, economic, and political conditions, Americans once again engaged in widespread dissent and protest, particularly during the 1880s and 1890s. These two decades were characterized by attacks, frequently violent, on the "industrial complex"—big business—which was depicted as having a stranglehold on the country. Attempts to organize workers and strengthen the power of labor led to cries of socialism, Communism, and anarchism. Frequently such efforts resulted in violence, as evidenced by the Haymarket Riot (1886), the Homestead Strike (1892), and the Pullman Strike (1894).

Agricultural discontent was also widespread as farmers rose in protest against taxes, transportation costs (i.e., the railroads), declining prices, and a "hard" money policy. It was at this time that a third party was formed known as the Populist party, a party which author Clinton Rossiter has suggested was the only genuine example in America's history of a true minor party, a dissident movement with the ingredients of a potential major party.

These decades also witnessed the famous march of Coxey's Army on Washington, D.C., and attacks on high unemployment, massive political corruption in cities, and affluence and its effects. They also witnessed calls for the relief of slum conditions and poverty, demands for women's rights, most particularly the right to vote, and renewed attacks against alcohol. In addition, anti-black, anti-Catholic, and anti-immigrant feelings were strong. Hence, as historians Richard Hofstadter, William Miller, and Daniel Aaron noted in their *The American Republic:*

There were moments during the midnineties when one-half of the nation seemed on the march against infuriating abuses and the other half wringing its hands in fright over the rise of radicalism.

Dissent and protest activities, particularly those connected with workers and working conditions, continued into the twentieth century, the two decades following the end of World War I being decades of turmoil. The war and the major strikes that occurred shortly thereafter triggered great resentment and fear of Communists, socialists, anarchists, foreigners, and blacks. The Ku Klux Klan revived, and the anti-Communist Palmer Raids were launched. Famous trials such as the Scopes trial and the Sacco and Vanzetti trial mobilized factions of dissidents. Schools and school teachers became targets as efforts were made to insure their orthodoxy. The Great Depression and the New Deal of President Franklin D. Roosevelt; the formation of the Congress of Industrial Organizations (the CIO) and the resultant drive for unionization which often led to violent confrontations and use of new tactics such as the sit-down strike and lock-outs; personalities such as Huey Long, Father Charles Coughlin, Dr. Francis Townsend, and Marcus Garvey, and the development of groups sympathetic to fascism or communism all coalesced in these years.

Thus, from colonial beginnings, to years early in the nation's development, to the present decade, dissent and protest have deep roots in America. We again find ourselves in an era of massive dissent and protest reminiscent in a number of ways of earlier eras yet differing in important ways as well.

For example, recent dissent and protest activities have occurred during years of prosperity rather than years of economic depression. They have occurred in a society where information is rapidly dispersed, where television coverage makes it possible to publicize events more widely, thus exposing more people to these activities. Another characteristic is the increasing involvement of citizens under the age of thirty, particularly college students, in significant organizations and activities. The rapidly vanishing melting-pot theory is being replaced by an increasing emphasis upon ethnic awareness, by a large variety of ethnic groups making their voices heard in their drive for change, some to the exclusion of whites. An increasing number of middle-class citizens are involved—the haves of the society as opposed to the have-nots—and are engaged in what some have called a "qualitative revolution" (i.e., concern with the quality of life) side-by-side with others who are engaged in a more traditional "quantitative revolution" (i.e., concern with quantity, enough things in life).

Today we witness the decline of authority by traditional societal bulwarks such as the family, the church, the government, and the school, as each increasingly finds itself a target of dissent. This factor, coupled with the existence in America of unprecedented overall affluence, has opened the doors to alternative life-styles more widely perhaps than ever before.

As one surveys the past and observes the present, the persistence of dissent and protest in this country is unmistakable. We have a long tradition of dissent, a tradition that appears subject to periodic eruptions. Thus as one observes the present and projects into the future, he cannot easily dismiss this tradition. Change is and has been ever present in America. Change is never easy or smooth. It produces challenge and encourages dissent. The tradition of dissent and protest is one of the great legacies of our country. The great challenge may very well be this: "Given the present nature of our society, can we permit dissent and protest to flourish and still remain both free and a society?" Or, to put it yet another way, "Given the present nature of our society, can we remain both free and a society and not permit this tradition to flourish?"

Chapter 3

The Anatomy of

Contemporary Protest

Black Protest

During the 1950s many commentators on the American scene were critical of what they discerned as the "apathetic American." These "apathetic Americans," particularly those found on the nation's college and university campuses, were depicted as knowing little of the problems of the country and the world and, what was felt to be even more important, of caring even less about such problems. Obsessed with their own personal interests, namely their careers and material comforts, these Americans seemed to have as their only goal conformity to conventional societal roles and expectations.

Yet as placid as America may have appeared to some of those observers, strong currents of change were surging beneath that calm surface. Perhaps the strongest and most dominant of these currents was the development of black awareness and the growth of black militancy. The middle part of the 1950s witnessed the 1954 United States Supreme Court decision of *Brown v. Board of Education* and the 1955–1956 Montgomery bus boycott, two incidents which triggered what has alternately been described as "the Negro Revolt," "the civil rights movement," "the black liberation movement," "the Third World revolution," etc. A summary of some of the major incidents in the growth of black militancy from 1960 to 1972 is provided in Table 3.1.

A perusal of this table is instructive, for it reveals various approaches, various leaders and groups, various gains, and various setbacks of recent black protest. It also suggests some of the problems still confronting the black citizen in America.

Table 3.1. Major Incidents in the Growth of Black Militancy, 1960 to 1973

Year	Incident
1960	Sit-ins begin in Greensboro, N.C., stimulating the growth of the Student Nonviolent Coordinating Committee (SNCC).
1961	The Congress of Racial Equality (CORE) organizes the "Freedom Rides" to test segregation in interstate facilities.
1962	James Meredith enters the University of Mississippi, sparking a campus riot.
1963	Authorities use police dogs and fire hoses on demonstrators in Birmingham, Alabama. Medgar Evers, Mississippi state chairman of the NACCP, dies after being shot by a sniper in front of his home. Demonstrations begin in northern cities protesting *de facto* segregation. Four young black girls die while attending Sunday School when their church is bombed. Dr. Martin Luther King, Jr., leads over 200,000 demonstrators in a Washington, D.C., "Freedom March."
1964	The bodies of civil-rights workers James Chaney, Andrew Goodman, and Michael Schwerner are found. They had been shot and beaten. New York City announces a busing plan to eliminate *de facto* segregation in city schools. Riots break out in Harlem and other northern cities. Congress passes the 1964 Civil Rights Law, which includes key provisions relating to public accommodations, school integration, employment, and voter registration.
1965	Malcolm X is assassinated in New York City. Selma, Alabama, marches produce violence as the Rev. James Reeb and Mrs. Viola Luizzo die in related incidents. The Watts riot erupts, resulting in the deaths of 35 people and damages in excess of $220 billion. Congress passes the Voting Rights Law of 1965.
1966	James Meredith is shot from ambush while on a march to urge blacks to register and vote. Riots break out in various cities including Chicago, New York, Cleveland, and Jacksonville. Stokely Carmichael popularizes the cry of "black power."
1967	Four-day national black-power conference held in Newark, N.J. Dr. Martin Luther King, Jr., calls for a boycott of the Vietnam war by all men of conscience. Major riots break out, the most severe of which occur in Newark, N.J., and Detroit, Michigan.

Table 3.1. Major Incidents in the Growth of Black Militancy (cont.)

Year	Incident
1968	The National Advisory Commission on Civil Disorders (the Kerner Commission) issues its report on the 1967 riots. Dr. Martin Luther King, Jr., is assassinated in Memphis. Racial violence erupts in over 100 cities following news of Dr. King's death. Poor People's March on Washington led by Ralph Abernathy establishes "Resurrection City" on Capitol grounds. Two black Olympic stars give the clenched-fist, black-power salute while on the victory stand. Congress passes the Civil Rights Law of 1968 providing for fair-housing standards on the sale and rental of 80 percent of housing in the United States.
1969	Black-studies programs are instituted on a number of the nation's college and university campuses. FBI Director J. Edgar Hoover charges that the Black Panthers represent "the greatest threat to the internal security of the country" among black extremist groups. Violence and small-scale riots erupt in cities across the nation. Two Black Panther party leaders die in police raid on party headquarters in the city of Chicago. The Supreme Court unanimously rules that school districts must end segregation "at once."
1970	Pres. Nixon announces his opposition "to any compulsory busing of people beyond normal geographic school zones for the purpose of achieving racial balance." Two black students are killed during disturbances on the Jackson State College campus. Frequent clashes occur between law officials and the Black Panthers in cities such as New York, Philadelphia, Chicago, etc.
1971	Thirteen members of the House of Representatives form the "Congressional Black Caucus." The Supreme Court rules that busing is a constitutionally permissible tool to achieve desegregated schools. National Urban League leader Whitney Young accidentally drowns. Whites protesting busing engage in boycotts and acts of violence. Pres. Nixon indicates he will enforce existing laws against racial discrimination in housing but he will not force communities to accept low- and/or moderate-income housing projects. The U.S. Commission on Civil Rights accuses the Nixon Administration of inadequate enforcement of the nation's civil-rights laws. Significant dissension appears amid the ranks of the Black Panthers. Jesse Jackson leaves the Southern Christian Leadership Conference (SCLC) and forms Operation PUSH.

Table 3.1. Major Incidents in the Growth of Black Militancy (cont.)

Year	Incident
1972	Angela Davis is acquitted in California trial. Black leaders Jackie Robinson and Adam Clayton Powell die. Racism in the armed services becomes an issue of national concern.
1973	Thomas Bradley elected as the first black mayor of Los Angeles, the nation's third largest city. Black Panther Bobby Seale wins run-off spot for mayor of Oakland though he loses in subsequent election. After announcing his intention to resign as president of the SCLC, Ralph Abernathy reverses his decision and agrees to remain in office.

Table 3.1 begins with the year 1960 and the start of the sit-in movement. While the sit-in type of protest was not invented in 1960 (author Herbert Aptheker reports that the technique was employed by a Negro slave as far back as the early seventeenth century), the sit-in technique was revived and given new vigor by the four North Carolina A & T students who staged a sit-in protest on February 1, 1960, in a Greensboro, North Carolina, store. This incident inspired similar protests and the technique rapidly spread. In assessing the significance of the sit-in movement, the National Advisory Commission on Civil Disorders (popularly referred to as the Kerner Commission) wrote:

> The Negro protest movement would never be the same again. The Southern college students shook the power structure of the Negro community, made direct action temporarily pre-eminent as a civil rights tactic, speeded up the process of social change in race relations, and ultimately turned the Negro protest organizations toward a deep concern with the economic and social problems of the masses.
>
> Involved in this was a gradual shift in both tactics and goals: from legal to direct action, from middle and upper class to mass action, from attempts to guarantee the Negro's constitutional rights to efforts to secure economic policies giving him equality of opportunity in a changing society, from appeals to the sense of fair play of white Americans to demands based upon power in the black ghetto.

The success of the student movement threatened existing Negro leadership and precipitated a spirited rivalry among civil rights organizations.

Before 1960 the National Association for the Advancement of Colored People (NAACP), an organization that by the end of 1971 claimed a multiracial membership in excess of 400,000, was the primary force for change. Essentially appealing to both blacks and whites of middle- and upper-class standing, the NAACP sought to end racial discrimination through legal action and public education. The Southern Christian Leadership Conference (SCLC), a loose-knit organization formed in 1957 in response to the Montgomery bus boycott and originally headed by Dr. Martin Luther King, Jr., favored nonviolent direct action characterized by personal involvement. These two organizations in conjunction with two others, the Congress of Racial Equality (CORE) and the Student Nonviolent Coordinating Committee (SNCC), provided the major impetus throughout the first half of the 1960s.

However, as concern shifted from overt *de jure* segregation in the South to the more subtle *de facto* segregation of the North, as white resistance hardened and grew more violent, serious reexamination of the nature and goals of black protest steadily grew. The "black power" slogan popularized by Stokely Carmichael symbolized this process and revealed the factionalism within the black protest movement. Some groups such as the NAACP and the SCLC continued to press for integration and assimilation. Other groups, CORE and the Black Muslims among them, called for black nationalism or separatism, either the formation of a separate nation with several designated all-black states or the strengthening of the segregated black community politically, economically, and culturally with the implementation of black control of black communities. Still others, like the Black Panthers, espoused Marxist rhetoric and advocated a revolutionary solution to the problems confronting black Americans.

Following the tragic assassination in 1968 of the disciple of nonviolence, Dr. Martin Luther King, Jr., the factionalism of the black movement was underscored. No one individual has been able to assume the position of preeminence that Dr. King held. In fact, most observers believe the emergence of such a figure would be unlikely owing to the diverse nature of black interests and goals. Such leaders as Roy Wilkins of the NAACP, Roy

Innis of CORE, Jesse Jackson of PUSH, Ralph Abernathy of the SCLC, and Huey Newton of the Black Panthers attest to that diversity.

With the decline of large-scale civil disturbances and radical organizations like the Black Panthers, issues of school desegregation, fair-employment practices, and the building and location of low-income and middle-income housing came into prominence in the early 1970s. Assessing the significance of the year 1971, black sociologist Charles V. Hamilton has written in *The Americana Annual, 1972*, in an article entitled "Race Relations":

> The era ahead is likely to be less violent and more political, at least on the part of blacks and other minorities. But it might be that some white groups, in an attempt to counter the minorities' demands and policies, will become more prone to violence and massive resistance.

Black protest has played a most important and significant role in the United States. Not only has it served as an impetus for black citizens, but the principles for which blacks have fought, the tactics that blacks have used, and the nature of American society black protest has exposed have been educative for many other Americans. Black protest has, in effect, served a catalytic function by stimulating other types of protest ranging from student protest, to anti-war protest, to feminist protest, to Chicano, Indian, and other minority-group protest.

Student Protest

In addition to black protest, two other types of protest— student protest and anti-war protest—dominated the decade of the 1960s. (Table 3.2 and Table 3.6 contain summaries of major incidents in these two protest movements.) If the appearance of black militancy surprised a number of Americans, the development and course of student activism and anti-war protest shocked them. And while related and often intertwined, student protest and anti-war protest provide unique and significant dimensions to the character of dissent and protest in the United States.

The 1964 Berkeley Free Speech Movement stood as a protest to the depersonalized and bureaucratic trends of the "megaversity," a "knowledge factory" characterized by the application of industrial techniques to university life (i.e., large assembly-line-

Table 3.2. Major Incidents in the Growth of Student Activism, 1960 to 1973

Year	Incident
1960	Four black students at North Carolina A & T initiate the modern sit-in movement.
1961	5,000 Ohio State students march to protest faculty rejection of a Rose Bowl bid.
1962	Students for a Democratic Society (SDS) hold an organizational meeting in Port Huron, Michigan. Rioting breaks out at the University of Mississippi in an attempt to prevent James Meredith, the first black student, from entering. A Washington, D.C., peace march marks the first national student demonstration in decades.
1964	The Mississippi Summer project to register black voters enlists the participation of many students. The "Free Speech Movement" led by Mario Savio erupts on the Berkeley, California, campus.
1965	20,000 students participate in a SDS-sponsored student march protesting the Vietnam war. Teach-ins begin on various campuses across the nation. General Hershey of the Selective Service announces that some students will be drafted and asks that universities and colleges cooperate by furnishing class-rank information.
1966	Brown University students hold the first protest against recruiters for Dow Chemical, a napalm manufacturer. The presence of military, CIA, and Dow Chemical recruiters stimulates protests on many college and university campuses.
1968	A number of major demonstrations begin at various institutions. Columbia University uprisings led by Mark Rudd and the SDS feature the seizure of buildings, the holding of hostages, and the use of police on campus. Major protests occur at Harvard University in opposition to the ROTC program. Students release letters revealing links between Harvard and the CIA.
1969	Cornell University students stage protests and emerge from a seized building carrying armed weapons. Berkeley, California, witnesses the "People's Park" incident. National Guardsmen exchange gunfire with students at North Carolina A & T University. Major disturbances occur on many campuses, including those at the University of Wisconsin, Harvard, and M.I.T. Various states pass laws restricting financial assistance to students engaging in campus disruption.

Table 3.2. Major Incidents in the Growth of Student Activism (cont.)

Year	Incident
1970	National Guardsmen shoot four students to death on the campus of Kent State University. State policemen shoot to death two students on the Jackson State College campus and fire into a dormitory. A bomb explosion at the University of Wisconsin kills one, injures three others, and extensively damages the Army Mathematics Research Center. Radicals admit to the act. Many colleges and universities close for a period of time in the fall to permit students to become actively involved in the November elections.
1971	Fires and firebombings cause extensive damage at the University of California at Santa Cruz, Tufts University, etc. Major demonstrations at the Universities of Wisconsin and Maryland necessitate the use of outside forces to restore order. Stolen FBI documents reveal large-scale surveillance of student, black, and anti-war groups. The 26th Amendment is passed, giving 18- to 20-year-olds the right to vote in all elections.
1972	Major disturbances erupt on many campuses, including universities in Michigan, Minnesota, Wisconsin, New Mexico, and Florida. Disturbances at Southern University result in the death of two students, and the university is closed to prevent further violence.
1973	Student strike closes Antioch College.

like lecture halls, the use of numbers instead of names, and so on). Demonstrating the value of direct action, the interrelationship between the university and the larger society, and the powerlessness of university officials to respond effectively, the Free Speech Movement proved to be a major turning point in the development of student activism.

Table 3.2 indicates the growth and escalation of student activism after 1964, from the nonviolent protest of the FSM at Berkeley, to the violence at Columbia University and San Francisco State in 1968, to the deaths at Kent State University and Jackson State College in 1971 and Southern University in 1972. Studies dealing with the extent of student activism provide further evidence of its spread. For example, according to Jerome Skolnick in *The Politics of Protest,* a National Student Association study counting only those demonstrations involving 35 students or more revealed that for the first half of the

1967–1968 academic year there were 71 separate demonstrations on 62 campuses, and for the second half the number of demonstrations increased to 221 at 101 schools. A survey of the 1969–1970 academic year conducted by Alexander Astin and reported by him in the *Educational Record* was based on student newspapers from 223 separate institutions and found 1,493 distinct protest incidents. Using a statistically weighted estimate for the 2,429 American colleges and universities, Astin estimated that there were more than 9,400 separate protest incidents on American campuses during the 1969–1970 academic year.

Educational historian Lawrence Cremin has suggested in an article in *The 1969 World Book Year Book* that student rebellion in the United States has roots as deep as the seventeenth century, citing an incident in which Harvard University students successfully forced the resignation of Harvard's President. Philip Altbach and Patti Peterson in "Before Berkeley: Historical Perspectives on American Student Activism" report antecedents dating to 1823, when students engaged in disruptive activity at Harvard University. They note, however, that "student activism before 1960 . . . had no major impact on national policy, and prior to 1900, no organized student activist groups emerged." Thus, the 1960s and particularly the Berkeley Free Speech Movement mark a critical stage in the development of student activism in the United States.

The appearance of large numbers of demonstrations brought forth many questions about the characteristics of the individuals who were involved. Commissions investigating campus disruptions have generally painted a favorable portrait of student activists. For example, the Cox Commission report, *Crisis at Columbia,* on the 1968 spring disturbances at that institution found:

> The present generation of young people in our universities is the best informed, the most intelligent, and the most idealistic this country has ever known. This is the experience of teachers everywhere.
>
> It is also the most sensitive to public issues and the most sophisticated in political tactics. Perhaps because they enjoy the affluence to support their ideals, today's undergraduate and graduate students exhibit, as a group, a higher level of social conscience than preceding generations.

The ability, social consciousness and conscience, political sensitivity, and honest realism of today's students are a prime cause of student disturbances. . . . That they seemingly can do so little to correct the wrongs through conventional political discourse tends to produce in the most idealistic and energetic students a strong sense of frustration.

An analysis of studies probing personal backgrounds and characteristics reveals a fairly clear and consistent profile of the student activist. Obviously there are dangers in attempting to name a "typical" or "average" anything. It must be remembered that the following characteristics form a composite of the student activist. Not every student activist possesses each and every one of these characteristics; rather, most student activists possess most of these characteristics. Hence, while caution must be exercised in the use of such a composite, such profiles of groups involved in various activities are often valuable in attempts to understand particular forms of behavior.

With these considerations in mind, then, reflect on the social and psychological characteristics indicated in Table 3.3. At least one characteristic in each category has been found to typify the student activist. Using your own impressions and judgment, select one from each of the categories in the table to form a profile of the "typical" student activist.

Most studies indicate that activist students come from upper-middle-class, affluent families living in large urban areas. Their fathers tend to be successful professional men, men to whom formal educational achievement has been important. Student activists tend to come from families who have "made it" in American society, from families with the status to provide the social and economic security so often deemed necessary for independence of thought and action.

These studies further suggest a strong continuity between student activists and their parents. Rather than being in open rebellion against the values and political orientations of their parents, student activists tend to come from families who are liberal, who have leftist political leanings, and who, when they do identify with a political party, tend to identify with the Democratic party rather than the Republican party. And while student activists may be more idealistic and committed than their parents, the differences are frequently ones of degree rather than of substance.

Table 3.3. Student Activist Profile

I. Family Background

A. Socio-Economic Level
   (1) Upper middle class
   (2) Middle class
   (3) Lower middle class
   (4) Lower class
B. Place of Residence
   (1) Large urban area (more than 500,000 inhabitants)
   (2) Small urban area (between 100,000 to 250,000 residents)
   (3) Suburban area
   (4) Rural area
C. Father's Occupation
   (1) Businessman
   (2) Professional (lawyer, doctor, etc.)
   (3) Skilled worker
   (4) Unskilled worker
D. Parents' Political Background
   (1) Conservative Republican
   (2) Liberal Republican
   (3) Liberal Democrat
   (4) Conservative Democrat

II. Personal Characteristics

E. Intellectual Orientations
   (1) Social sciences (sociology, psychology, etc.)
   (2) Physical sciences (chemistry, physics, etc.)
   (3) Applied sciences (engineering, etc.)
   (4) Humanities (literature, music, art, etc.)
F. Academic Achievement
   (1) Relatively high—a good student
   (2) Average—an average student
   (3) Underachiever—a poor student
   (4) Little ability—a poor student

Most student activists tend to come from homes in which permissive child-rearing practices have been employed. Thus as children student activists have been given considerable latitude to develop their own life-styles and values as opposed to other homes in which a more rigid value system has been imposed.

More often academically talented, above-average students, student activists tend to be intellectually oriented, seeing themselves as intellectuals and thus regarding education as an end in itself rather than merely as a means of acquiring the proper credentials for material success. Activist students also tend to major in the social sciences or the humanities, as opposed to the physical or applied sciences, and consequently concentrate academically on the nature of society and relationships within it, frequently from a critical perspective.

One of the more interesting of the studies of student activists is that conducted by M. Brewster Smith which uses a list of descriptive words or phrases from which students are asked to select those that best describe themselves. Table 3.4 provides an opportunity to become familiar with this technique and engage in a kind of personal inventory. Before reading further, take a few minutes to compose a self-profile using Table 3.4.

Table 3.4. Personal Inventory: How Do You See Yourself?

From the following list, select at least ten words or phrases that best describe you as you perceive yourself to be.

Ambitious	Artistic	Aware
Competitive	Conventional	Creative
Doubting	Frank	Free
Foresightful	Idealistic	Imaginative
Impulsive	Likes to be best	Orderly
Perceptive	Plans ahead	Practical
Rebellious	Responsible	Self-controlled
Self-denying	Sensitive	Sociable

While Smith used a great many more entries than those appearing in this table, those used here were among those which Smith found to distinguish between activists and nonactivists rather than those which were rated highest by each group. On the basis of Smith's findings, activists were most likely to see themselves as artistic, aware, creative, doubting, frank, free, idealistic, imaginative, impulsive, perceptive, rebellious, and sensitive. Nonactivists, on the other hand, were most likely to describe themselves as ambitious, competitive, conventional, foresightful, likes to be best, orderly, plans ahead, practical, responsible, self-controlled, self-denying, and sociable. Smith concluded that nonactivist students appear to embody those qualities which comprise the Protestant Ethic, whereas activist students seem to adhere to humanistic, anti-Protestant Ethic values, oftentimes referred to as those of the counterculture. (How does your profile compare to these results?)

One of the more prevalent and widely circulated views is that student activists constitute an extremely small percentage of college youth. Yet studies in this area suggest that this may be a misconception, for a significant degree of support for student-activist values has been found to exist in various studies.

Following the decision to send United States combat troops into Cambodia, a large number of demonstrations and protests erupted on college and university campuses across this country, the most famous of which occurred at Kent State University in Ohio. In their attempt to discover both the extent and the significance of campus protest activities, the American Council on Education commissioned the Louis Harris organization to conduct a survey of student attitudes at the nation's colleges and universities. The survey was taken in June 1970 and consisted of interviews with 820 full-time undergraduate students randomly selected in a cross section of 50 colleges and universities.

According to the Harris survey (Fig. 3.1), 48 percent of undergraduate students—virtually one out of every two—took part in demonstrations or protests at their schools following the sending of United States troops to Cambodia. And 75 percent—three out of every four—indicated that they favored the goals of such protests and demonstrations, while only 16 percent indicated opposition. Other findings of interest include responses to the question, "Have demonstrations been an effective form of protest, have they been ineffective, or have they done more harm

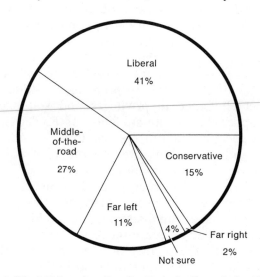

Fig. 3.1. Political Philosophy: How Do Students Characterize Themselves?

than good?" Of those queried, 57 percent felt demonstrations had been an effective form of protest, while 19 percent felt they had been an ineffective form of protest and 20 percent felt demonstrations had done more harm than good.

When asked whether demonstrations and protests should continue or whether other means of bringing about change would be more effective, the students indicated some uncertainty, for 47 percent felt demonstrations and protests should continue while 47 percent felt other means should be used.

Will protest and radical action effect social change in the United States system? When asked that question, 66 percent of those queried felt change will be speeded up by such action, 13 percent felt change will be slowed down, 12 percent felt it will have no effect, and 9 percent had no opinion.

Finally, when asked if they believed the United States had become a highly repressive society, intolerant of dissent, 58 percent responded "yes" while 39 percent disagreed. All of these Harris findings are from the 1970 publication, *A Survey of the Attitudes of College Students.*

While the legacy of the black protest movement to the student and anti-war protest movements is clear and unmistakable, important differences appear between them. Black involvement in the anti-war movement has been noticeably lacking and black student protest seems distinct from white student protest. Many of these differences may be attributable to a fundamental difference in goals. Black student activists, primarily those from urban ghetto backgrounds, have goals which often transcend the campus and share close identification with the more concrete goals of the black protest movement, while white student activism is characterized by less clearly defined goals. Consequently, in some respects black student activism offers a direct challenge to privileges and status enjoyed by middle- and upper-class white students. As Frederick W. Obear has noted, "Colleges and universities thus became the place where a new and less submissive generation of ethnic minorities vented its rage at white-dominated society."

Kenneth Keniston has suggested in an article in the *New York Times Magazine* that student activism represents a fusion of two revolutions, each with distinct goals and historical origins. One of these he termed a "quantitative revolution," a movement concerned "less with the quality of life than with the amount of political freedom, the quantity and distribution of goods or the amount and level of injustice." Finding this "a combination of the old and familiar revolution of the industrial society, the liberal-democratic-egalitarian revolution that started in America and France at the time of the 18th century . . . ," Keniston concluded that it is this revolution in which black militancy is deeply rooted.

On the other hand, Keniston pointed to a second type of revolution, a "qualitative revolution," the product of the post-industrial twentieth century. It is this revolution that engages much of the white student activists, for to a great extent they have already achieved the goals of the "quantitative revolution." They appear to be concerned less with social, economic, or political goals than with psychological, historical, and cultural goals, goals which are often nebulous and unarticulated and which frequently include emphasis upon direct personal experience, individuality, creativity, participatory democracy, and the freedom to create new life-styles and values.

Keniston cautioned, however, that such distinctions are rarely made by student activists, that "in any one situation the two revolutions are joined and fused, if not confused," and that "in all student movements, these revolutions co-exist in uneasy and often abrasive tension."

Anti-War Protest

Frequently overlapping with student activism has been the development of the Vietnam anti-war movement in the United States, for in a very real sense the American university has played a role of central importance in anti-war dissent. Encompassing far more than the nation's campuses, however, the anti-war movement in the United States marks a unique chapter in American dissent. In some two hundred years of American existence, no movement similar to the broad-based nature of the Vietnam anti-war movement has appeared. For while one can point to some examples of war protest, such as those in the Mexican War, in World War I, and in World War II, the nature of that protest was marginal and rather easily dismissed. Such is not the case, however, with the Vietnam anti-war movement, for it takes in a substantial part of the American populace and has had a significant impact on the development of government policy.

Some have suggested that the Vietnam anti-war movement is a conspiracy directed by Communists, a theory that has also been advanced to explain both the growth of black militancy and the growth of student activism. Others, however, suggest that while prominent leaders do appear, their actual influence is minimal, for the movement is more dependent upon outside events than it is upon the control of any leader or group. The Task Force on Demonstrations, Protests, and Group Violence, commonly referred to as the Skolnick Commission, has suggested:

> the peace movement does have some broad continuities and tendencies, well understood by most prominent leaders, but . . . its loosely participatory, unstructured aspect can scarcely be overestimated. . . .
>
> The more one learns about the organizational structure and development of the peace movement, the more reluctant one must be to speak of its concerted direction. . . . [T]he movement has been and remains in a posture of responding to events outside its control; the chief milestones in its growth have been its days of widespread outrage at escalations, bombing resumptions, draft policies, and prosecutions.

Table 3.5 gives a brief summary of major events in the conduct of the Vietnam war and Table 3.6 provides an outline of major events in the anti-war movement. Used in conjunction with Table 2.1 and Table 3.2, they offer support for the conclusion reached by the Skolnick Commission that the development of the anti-war movement is greatly dependent upon the events of the Vietnam war. For example, as peace possibilities neared, as evidenced by President Johnson's speech in March 1968 and by Henry Kissinger's "Peace is at hand" speech in October 1972, the fervor of anti-war protest declined. Following major escalations in Vietnam, such as President Nixon's decision to send American troops into Cambodia in 1970, the tenor of the anti-war movement increased.

A number of factors have combined to produce the degree of anti-war sentiment prevalent in the past decade. One of the most basic of these factors is the nature of the war itself. Fought in a remote, little-understood area of Southeast Asia in an unconventional guerrilla fashion, the war was slow to creep into the consciousness of the American public. The Gulf of Tonkin incident in August 1964, during a Presidential campaign, brought the war into sharper focus, particularly after Lyndon Johnson, who had been thought of as the "peace candidate," rapidly escalated the war in 1965.

Table 3.5. Major Incidents in American Involvement in Vietnam, 1954 to 1973

Year	Incident
1954	French forces are defeated at the battle of Dienbienphu. The Geneva Accords are signed providing for the future of the area formerly known as French Indochina. The United States and seven other nations join in signing the SEATO alliance. President Eisenhower sends a letter to Ngo Dinh Diem promising American assistance to the State of Vietnam (i.e., South Vietnam).
1956	Elections to unify Vietnam as provided by the 1954 Geneva Accords are not held.
1960	The United States begins to replace civilian advisors with military advisors.
1963	Ngo Dinh Diem, leader of South Vietnam, is murdered in a *coup d'état*. A series of governments rises and falls in a succession of *coups d'état*.
1964	President Johnson announces on national television that North Vietnam has attacked American ships in the Gulf of Tonkin. Congress passes the Gulf of Tonkin Resolution authorizing President Johnson to "take all necessary measures to repel any armed attack against the forces of the United States and to prevent further aggression."
1965	United States planes begin combat missions over North Vietnam. American troops increase to almost 200,000 by the end of the year compared to approximately 20,000 at the beginning of the year.
1966	American troops continue to increase, the number reaching nearly 400,000 by the end of the year.
1967	American troops number in excess of 500,000. Nguyen Van Thieu is elected President and Nguyen Cao Ky is elected Vice President in South Vietnam.
1968	Communist forces launch the Tet Offensive early in the year. President Johnson announces his decision not to seek reelection. In the same speech, he announces his decision to stop bombing above the 20th parallel and asks that peace negotiations begin. Preliminary peace talks begin in Paris, France. Incident later known as the My Lai massacre occurs.
1969	Substantive peace talks are initiated among the United States, South Vietnam, North Vietnam, and the Vietcong. President Nixon announces his Vietnamization plan designed to end the war. North Vietnamese leader, Ho Chi Minh, dies at the age of 79.

Table 3.5. Major Incidents in American Involvement in Vietnam (cont.)

Year	Incident
1970	President Nixon continues to withdraw American troops from Vietnam. President Nixon announces that United States forces have engaged in operations in Cambodia.
1971	The New York *Times* prints the first installment of the "Pentagon Papers." Government efforts to prevent further publication fail when the United States Supreme Court rules 6–3 in favor of continued publication. Running unopposed, Nguyen Van Thieu is reelected President of South Vietnam. United States forces continue to be withdrawn from Vietnam.
1972	President Nixon announces the mining of all North Vietnamese waterways. Amid rumors of progress at the peace talks, Presidential advisor announces that "peace is at hand." The United States unleashes a massive aerial bombardment in North Vietnam, using B-52's over Hanoi for the first time in the war.
1973	Cease-fire agreement for Vietnam signed in Paris on January 27. With the release of U.S. POW's, all U.S. combat forces are withdrawn from South Vietnam. United States continues to bomb in Cambodia until August 15. A Senate investigation reveals that U.S. secretly engaged in over 3,600 bombing missions in Cambodia during 1969 and 1970.

As the level of fighting increased, so did the amount of attention focused on the conflict increase. Teach-ins held on college and university campuses pointed to the dubious nature of American involvement. So, too, did the number of critical books and magazine articles that began to appear, detailing the controversial nature of American involvement. And criticism by such international figures as Secretary General U Thant of the United Nations and President Charles de Gaulle of France raised further doubts regarding the credibility of the American effort.

Concomitant with these were the tactics employed by American and South Vietnamese forces, tactics that included torture, napalm, destruction of villages, extensive bombing, and the use of chemical warfare including defoilants, herbicides, gas, etc. These facts were brought into the American home in daily newspapers and on television.

Table 3.6. Major Incidents in the Growth of Anti-war Protest, 1965 to 1973

Year	Incident
1965	Teach-ins begin on many of the nation's college and university campuses. Anti-war demonstrations with crowds in excess of 10,000 are held in major cities across the nation. Demonstrators attempt to block troop trains in Oakland and Berkeley, California.
1966	Campus demonstrations erupt in protest against military and war-related industry recruiters. Harrison Salisbury of the New York *Times* goes to North Vietnam and reports on the effects of American bombing on the people of that area.
1967	Major demonstrations are held in many of the nation's cities and in Washington, D.C. Selective Service Director, General Hershey, recommends that local draft boards reclassify unruly demonstrators. Dr. Martin Luther King, Jr., announces his opposition to the Vietnam war and calls upon men of conscience to boycott the war.
1968	Eugene McCarthy's campaign for the Democratic Presidential nomination attracts many anti-war people. Major demonstrations, connected with anti-war protest, erupt at various institutions, notably Columbia University. Major demonstrations and violence disrupt the Democratic National Convention in Chicago. Dr. Benjamin Spock, the Rev. William Sloane Coffin, and several others are indicted for conspiracy to encourage draft evasion. The Rev. Philip Berrigan, the Rev. Daniel Berrigan, and others are arrested for burning draft records in Catonsville, Maryland. For the first time, the Gallup poll reveals that a majority of Americans oppose United States policy in Vietnam.
1969	Major demonstrations against continuation of the war continue, with participants in some of these exceeding 100,000. The year of the "moratoria." The United States Senate ·passes the Cooper-Church amendment limiting American involvement in Indochina.
1970	Following incidents of violence at Kent State and Jackson State, over 100 colleges and universities close in a massive protest. Major anti-war demonstrations continue. The Chicago 7 trial is held in Chicago, Illinois.
1971	Publication of the "Pentagon Papers." Demonstrations continue, highlighted by the "May Day" protests involving well over 100,000 in Washington, D.C., and resulting in the arrest of more than 12,000 people.

Table 3.6. Major Incidents in the Growth of Anti-war Protest (cont.)

Year	Incident
1972	President Nixon's decision to mine North Vietnamese harbors triggers major demonstrations on college campuses and in major cities. Small-scale demonstrations are held in various U.S. cities in protest to American bombing raids in December.
1973	Congress forces President Nixon to end U.S. bombing of Cambodia by August 15.

Added to this was the chaotic state of affairs in South Vietnam—the game of musical chairs following the assassination of Ngo Dinh Diem, the corruption of the South Vietnamese government, the dubious reputation and heavy desertion rate of South Vietnamese troops, the suppression of neutralist opposition, and the questionable "free" elections. Many Americans found such information bewildering and inconsistent with their ideas of "preserving freedom."

And, as the Skolnick Commission noted:

During the period of the Vietnam war there were other developments within the structure of American society that gave impetus to radical dissent. The racial polarization described in the report of the Kerner Commission assumed frightening proportions, and was worsened by the diversion of "Great Society" funds into war spending. The major political parties did not prove very responsive to sentiment for peace, and when a strong third party arose it drew strength from race hatred and sword-rattling. The Vietnam expenditures, which had possibly averted a recession in 1965, later contributed to a serious inflation. Moreover, critics felt that because of war expenditures, problems of conservation, traffic and pollution were neglected. Assassination haunted our public life, and contributed to the feeling of despair and frustration which affected many in the anti-war movement. Universities, the unofficial headquarters of the peace movement, were hampered by Federal research cutbacks and shaken by student protest which often focused on such war related activities as the development of biological warfare weapons.

Members of the Skolnick Commission have provided a detailed and valuable analysis of the social bases of the anti-war movement. In their analysis, they found the movement to be characterized according to social rather than organizational lines, composed primarily of middle-class professional and preprofessional students. And they noted with some exceptions, the striking absence of the rank-and-file American workingman in the anti-war movement. In fact, the American workingman became a symbolic figure, the "hard-hat," an outspoken supporter of Administration policy. Also notable in their absence, with the exception of leaders like Malcolm X and Dr. Martin Luther King, Jr., were black citizens on a mass basis.

Within the relatively well-educated, middle-class base, the anti-war movement received its principal support and leadership from three groups—teachers, students, and clergy. Teachers, primarily college and university professors, as well as other intellectuals played an important role in educating the public to the nature of the conflict. The importance of student involvement in the anti-war movement has already been alluded to and can be seen in Table 3.2. Clergymen, especially such figures as Dr. Martin Luther King, Jr., William Sloane Coffin, Philip and Daniel Berrigan, and Robert McAfee Brown, made important contributions to the anti-war movement.

In summary, the decade of the 1960s served to usher in a critical and in many ways unique era in American dissent and protest. Inspired by the growth and development of black protest, the student and anti-war protest movements subsequently developed in their own ways. The late 1960s showed further proliferation as other lines of dissent emerged, notably the feminist movement and the drive of other minorities for equality, including Indians, Chicanos, Puerto Ricans, etc.

Chapter 4

The Ethic of Dissent:

An Overview

The Ethic of Abe Fortas and Socrates

In many ways the year 1968 was a confusing and frightening year for many Americans. For 1968 was the year of the trial of Dr. Benjamin Spock, the Catonsville incident involving the Berrigan brothers, the "Poor People's March," and "Resurrection City"; the year of major demonstrations and violence at the Democratic National Convention in Chicago and on the campuses of Columbia University and San Francisco State University; the year of the assassinations of Robert Kennedy and Dr. Martin Luther King, Jr., and violent clashes in more than one hundred cities. It was also in that year that a book written by Abe Fortas, then an Associate Justice of the Supreme Court of the United States, appeared, a short but provocative book entitled, *Concerning Dissent and Civil Disobedience*.

In this book, Mr. Fortas affirmed the right of individuals to dissent and vigorously protest and noted that, despite his background as a lawyer and member of the Supreme Court, he hoped that he would have dissented, if he had lived in Hitler's Germany, by not obeying anti-Semitic edicts or, if he had lived in the South, by not obeying segregation ordinances. He then posed the following question:

> How, then, can I reconcile my profound belief in obedience to law and my equally basic need to disobey *these* laws? Is there a principle, a code, a theory to which a man, with honor and integrity, may subscribe? Or is it all a matter of individual judgment?

The problem Fortas posed is a common one, one worthy of further consideration. Is there an "ethic of dissent" to which one may subscribe or is it really only a matter of individual judgment?

Throughout history there are a number of incidents in which individuals have been engaged in various types of dissent with their society, incidents that may shed light on the question of the existence of an ethic of dissent. One of the classic examples of the individual in disagreement with his society is the dissent of Socrates. Socrates dedicated his life to the pursuit of knowledge and truth. Dubbed a "gadfly" because of his persistent efforts in this regard, Socrates probed beyond the simple approximations of truth professed by his fellow citizens and his government. His efforts angered a number of citizens and finally, when he was in his seventies, charges were brought against him for "reviling the gods, preaching other new gods, and corrupting the youth." At his trial, as recorded in Plato's "Apology," Socrates stood firm, refusing to compromise his principles or throw himself upon the mercy of the court, and when he was convicted and given the choice of banishment or death, Socrates chose death.

Shortly before he was to die, Socrates was visited early in the morning by one of his closest friends, Crito. The purpose of Crito's visit was to convince Socrates to escape and flee to another country. The following is loosely based on Plato's account of that meeting as found in the "Crito."

Socrates and Crito

CRITO: I've just received word that they've finally set the date. Tomorrow is scheduled to be the last day of your life.

SOCRATES: Well, if that is the will of God, I am willing to accept my fate.

CRITO: But why, Socrates? Please let me and your other friends help you to escape. Don't betray your own life when it might be saved, for that's only playing into the hands of your enemies. You must act now. The time for deliberation is over. You must escape and tonight has to be the night.

SOCRATES: Thank you for your concern, my friend. I appreciate your loyalty. You are indeed a true friend. But as you know, I am a man of reason and a man of principle. That is the essence of my life. I cannot betray them now. I want you to convince me to escape, but I'm afraid you will not be able to do so.

CRITO: But why? I don't understand.

SOCRATES: Let me ask you a simple question. Isn't it true that it is not life itself but a good life which is to be chiefly valued?

CRITO: Yes, I agree with that.

SOCRATES: And isn't it true that a good life is equivalent to a just and honorable life?

CRITO: Yes, it is.

SOCRATES: All right, then. In spite of what public opinion may say and in spite of the consequences, isn't it true that injustice is always an evil and that to act unjustly is to bring dishonor upon oneself?

CRITO: Yes, to act unjustly is to bring dishonor upon oneself.

SOCRATES: Then we must do no wrong?

CRITO: Of course I agree.

SOCRATES: And what of doing evil in return for evil—is that just or not?

CRITO: It is not just.

SOCRATES: Now, think about what you have just said. Do you really believe this, that we ought not to retaliate or do evil to anyone regardless of the evil we may have suffered because of him?

CRITO: Yes, I do.

SOCRATES: Now, should a man do what he knows is right, or should he do wrong, knowing it is wrong?

CRITO: He ought to do what he thinks is right, of course.

SOCRATES: Well? Don't you see, then, that if I escape, am I not really betraying my life's principles?

CRITO: I don't know. I'm confused.

SOCRATES: Let me put it another way. Some people argue that one does not have to obey a law if it is an unjust law, if the law imposes evil on himself or others, isn't that right?

CRITO: Some say that.

SOCRATES: But don't you see? We have an obligation to the state. After all, it is the state which has nurtured and educated us, which has provided the amenities of life for you and for me and for every other citizen. By remaining here and taking advantage of these opportunities, haven't we entered into at least an implied contract to obey the laws of the state? Aren't we obligated to obey its laws?

CRITO: But what if those laws are unjust?

SOCRATES: If you don't like the laws, you first have an obligation to persuade the state to change the laws. This is what I have tried to do. But, if you can't, you have one of two choices—either abide by the laws or leave the state. That's the choice.

CRITO: But Socrates, the state has sentenced you to die!

SOCRATES: Wait a minute. For over seventy years now I have lived in this state. I wasn't forced to remain here. I was free to leave but I chose to stay, to raise my children here. And I could have chosen banishment at my trial rather than remain here and face death. Should I back down now? Wouldn't that be turning my back upon agreements I have made as a citizen? By remaining here, haven't I agreed, at least tacitly, to be governed according to the state?

CRITO: But the state is planning to kill you!

SOCRATES: Crito, my friend, what good would it do to escape? Won't my friends also be punished for helping me to escape? Won't other governments see me as an enemy, as a subverter of laws? Isn't a corrupter of laws more than likely to be a corrupter of the young, the very crime the state has charged me with? And if this be true, what kind of country could I live in? Is existence worth having on those terms?

CRITO: No, no I guess not.

SOCRATES: All of my life I've stood for truth and justice. I've tried to help others in this way. Of what value is my life if I escape now?

No, Crito, I can't escape. Don't you see? I depart in innocence, a sufferer from and not a doer of evil; a victim not of laws but of men. I must stay and face my punishment.

The Socratic dissent ethic which emerges from the dialogue between Socrates and his friend, Crito, approximates the dissent ethic Abe Fortas details in his book. For Fortas as well as for Socrates, the legitimacy of the state is unquestioned as is the right of the state to make and enforce laws. Obedience to those laws is, in the words of Justice Fortas, "a moral as well as a legal imperative."

From the assumptions just stated, one might be led to an ethic typified by Adolf Eichmann, at least the Adolf Eichmann described by Hannah Arendt in her book, *Eichmann in Jerusalem: A Report on the Banality of Evil*. A member of Hitler's SS, Eichmann played an important role in the systematic extermination of Jews living in areas controlled by the Nazis. As the war neared its end, Eichmann had been able to flee Germany and take up residency in Argentina. It was in Argentina that he was seized by Israeli agents and brought back to Israel to stand trial in 1961 on charges of committing crimes against the Jewish people, crimes against humanity, and other war crimes. He was found guilty and sentenced to death.

In following the Eichmann trial, Dr. Arendt became convinced that Eichmann was not "a man obsessed with a dangerous and insatiable urge to kill," "a perverted, sadistic personality," but rather a "normal" person "neither feeble-minded nor indoctrinated nor cynical." Eichmann's crime was that of "being a good citizen," that is, of obeying specific orders he received in addition to the general laws of the state and working vigorously to carry them into execution. He dismissed, if he entertained any such feelings, attempts at dissent both on pragmatic and on philosophic grounds. Since he did not question the legitimacy of the state, he considered obedience to the law both expedient and imperative. Guided by such an ethic, Eichmann comes to share responsibility for genocide.

But Fortas has already explicitly rejected such an ethic as that followed by Eichmann, for he has suggested that if he had lived in Hitler's Germany, he hopes he would not have obeyed the anti-Jewish laws. Both Fortas and Socrates argue that there are laws and values of a higher order than state laws or values. Man has an obligation to do what he knows to be right, to refuse to comply with what he considers to be evil. If the state is wrong, man should use those processes provided by the state to change the laws or the situation. If, despite such efforts, a situation persists where a state law is immoral or malevolent, both men agree that compliance is not necessary. In that circumstance, however, when one finds that he cannot obey such laws and deliberately disobeys them, he must then be willing to accept the punishment society provides. For as Fortas argued in his book, "The motive of civil disobedience, whatever its type, does not confer immunity for law violation." By this ethic, dissent is permissible and even sometimes desirable, but it must be done within the societal framework, and it must be done with a willingness to accept punishment.

The Ethic of Martin Luther King, Jr.

The ethic typified by Dr. Martin Luther King, Jr., has much in common with the Socratic-Fortas ethic as previously described. Emphasizing the need for dissent, Dr. King asserted that a state passes two types of laws—just laws (i.e., "any law that uplifts human personality") and unjust laws (i.e., "any law that degrades human personality"). A citizen has a legal and moral obligation to obey just laws but a moral responsibility to disobey unjust laws. In fact, Dr. King contended that an unjust law is really no law at all and should be treated as such. He wrote in "Letter from Birmingham City Jail":

> I hope you can see the distinction I am trying to point out. In no sense do I advocate evading or defying the law as the rabid segregationist would do. This would lead to anarchy. One who breaks an unjust law must do it *openly, lovingly* . . . and with a willingness to accept the penalty. I submit that an individual who breaks a law that conscience tells him is unjust, and willingly accepts the penalty by staying in jail to arouse the conscience of the community over its injustice, is in reality expressing the very highest respect for law.

Where Dr. King departs somewhat from the Socratic-Fortas ethic is in his analysis of society and the means considered necessary to secure change. Dr. King contended in this same *Letter* that "freedom is never voluntarily given by the oppressor; it must be demanded by the oppressed." Hence, Dr. King has stood as the great champion of nonviolent direct action, a method that utilizes sit-ins, marches, picket lines, boycotts, etc., to create a crisis-like situation designed to force a community or state to confront the issue in question. "It seeks so to dramatize the issue that it can no longer be ignored."

At times the application of direct-action techniques has resulted in the violation of laws other than those considered in themselves to be unjust. For example, in protesting the issue of segregation, direct-action advocates have at times disobeyed valid court orders, blocked traffic or entry into public buildings, sat-in in the offices of public officials impeding their ability to function, etc. In such a situation, when dissenters refuse to obey valid laws as a means of protesting their opposition to other unjust laws or practices, Justice Fortas has raised strong reservations and reiterated the necessity to arrest and punish the dissenters.

At this point, consideration of the views of Henry David Thoreau suggests another dimension to a dissent ethic. Following his release from jail for failure to pay a Massachusetts poll tax because part of that money would be used to finance the Mexican War, Thoreau wrote what has become a classic essay,

"Civil Disobedience." His views of the state—"that government is best which governs not at all"—approach those of the anarchist, and his sentiments with respect to whether one owes primary allegiance to himself or to the law coincide with those of Socrates. Thoreau contended that if government "requires you to be an agent of injustice, then . . . break the law," for despite public opinion, if a man is right and his cause is just, he constitutes a majority of one and is justified in acting on his principles.

While most people tend to see Thoreau subscribing to an ethic of open, nonviolent dissent based on principles and characterized by a willingness to accept societal punishment for his acts of disobedience, at least one commentator (Harry Klaven in *Civil Disobedience: Theory and Practice*) has suggested that Thoreau "says nothing about what some of us take as a special morality in civil disobedience—the need to accept the punishment. He goes to jail, but he goes because he cannot figure out any way of getting out of going. He offers no theory about the propriety of going, or not going to jail; it just happens."

The Ethic of Howard Zinn

Whether one is willing to accept such an interpretation of Thoreau is debatable. What is of more value, however, is the suggestion that one need not necessarily accept the punishment of the state for acts based on just principles. This point is elaborated upon by Howard Zinn in *Disobedience and Democracy*, a book written as a reaction to the ethic set forth by Abe Fortas. Zinn argued that to accept punishment under unjust laws is equivalent to sanctioning and perpetuating injustice: it fails to help society discriminate between right and wrong. And, he added, when unjust laws and unjust punishments become the rule, "then the government and its officials *should* be toppled." He has written:

> But why was it right for Dr. King to accept an unjust verdict corroborating an unjust injunction, resulting in an unjust jail sentence. . . . ? Why should there not have been bitter, forceful complaint across the country against this set of oppressive acts? Is the general notion of obedience to law more important than the right of free assembly? Does quiet acceptance in such a case not merely perpetuate the notion that transgressions of justice by the government must be tolerated by citizens?

If the social function of protest is to change the unjust conditions of society, then that protest cannot stop with a court decision or a jail sentence. If the protest is morally justified (whether it breaks a law or not) it is morally justified to the very end, even past the point where a court has imposed a penalty. . . . How potent an effect can protest have if it stops dead in its tracks as soon as the very government it is criticizing decides against it?

Overall, Zinn raised nine questions with respect to the arguments of Abe Fortas, two more of which are of especial importance. Must the citizen limit his civil disobedience to only those laws that are themselves unjust or wrong, as Fortas has contended? Would such a position inevitably lead one to brand as unjustifiable protest actions by the poor, since poverty is not represented by specific laws?

Zinn has also taken issue with the question of whether civil disobedience must be absolutely nonviolent. To Fortas violence is an evil that is never defensible, particularly in an open society as found in the United States. But Zinn, after having defined civil disobedience as "the deliberate violation of law for a vital social purpose," refused to rule out the need for or use of violence in all situations and argued that in certain cases, such as self-defense or as a last resort to eliminate a great evil, violence may indeed be necessary.

The Ethic of Herbert Marcuse

The philosopher and influential spokesman of the New Left, Herbert Marcuse, provides insight into the question of the suitability of violence as a means of protest. An analysis of American society has led him to raise the issue of whether the United States is indeed an open society, a society in which all points of view are tolerated and permitted to be expressed. Marcuse has suggested that what exists is but an illusion of tolerance, an illusion that perpetuates already existing inequalities in the society. In a piece entitled "Postscript 1968 to 'Repressive Tolerance,'" he has stated:

Under the conditions prevailing in this country, tolerance does not, and cannot, fulfill the civilizing function attributed to it by the liberal protagonists of democracy, namely, protection of dissent. The progressive historical force of tolerance lies in its extension to those modes and forms of dissent which are not committed to the status quo of society, and not confined to the institutional framework of the established society. Consequently, the idea of tolerance implies the necessity, for the dissenting group or individuals, to become illegitimate if and when the established legitimacy prevents and counteracts the development of dissent. This would be the case not only in a totalitarian society . . . but also in a democracy. . . .

Marcuse believes that in the United States dissenters do not have an equal opportunity to present their views effectively because they are simply unable to afford the means to do so. The prohibitive cost of mass-media facilities, facilities controlled by the vested interests of the society, effectively prevents the circulation of dissenting views. Hence, Marcuse has proposed that what is needed is a form of "discriminating tolerance" to shift the balance between the vested interests of the majority and the dissent of the minority by

[doing] away with the sacred liberalistic principle of equality for "the other side" . . . where either there is no "other side" in any more than a formalistic sense, or where "the other side" is demonstrably "regressive" and impedes the possible improvement of the human condition.

In practice, this and similar analyses may help to explain why on some of the nation's campuses government spokesmen, particularly those speaking in defense of administrative policy in Vietnam, have been shouted down or prevented from speaking at all. It may further explain why, in recent years, we seem to be experiencing incidents ranging from increased heckling at political rallies and other public forums to increased incidents of the bombing of public buildings. Is the nature of American society such as to force dissenters to become increasingly more provocative and violent in order to receive media attention as a means of more widely disseminating their views?

The Relationship of Violence and Dissent

Regardless of how one responds to this question, it is clear that protest activities in recent years have, on some occasions, erupted with violence. Such violent clashes with governmental authorities have been termed "civil disturbances." Tables 4.1 and 4.2 detail the nature and extent of civil disturbances in the United States from the period of 1968 to early 1972, the first on the basis of section of the country and the latter by months or periods of the year.

Table 4.1. Civil Disturbances and Related Deaths, 1968 to 1971, By Section of the Country

Period	Total	Disturbances Major [1]	Serious [2]	Minor [3]	Related deaths
1968	435	26	54	355	83
North	107	6	11	90	21
South	113	9	20	84	16
Midwest	155	9	12	134	37
West	60	2	11	47	9
1969	245	8	49	188	19
North	55	3	15	37	5
South	57	2	11	44	3
Midwest	71	1	7	63	3
West	62	2	16	44	8
1970	195	18	58	119	33
North	41	4	7	30	2
South	41	5	7	29	9
Midwest	63	8	36	19	11
West	50	1	8	41	11
1971	39 [a]	10	29	x	10
North	4 [a]	0	4	x	0
South	14 [a]	6	8	x	5
Midwest	10 [a]	2	8	x	1
West	11 [a]	2	9	x	4

[1] Characterized by all of the following: (a) vandalism; (b) arson; (c) looting or gunfire; (d) outside police forces or troops used; (e) curfew imposed; (f) more than 300 people involved, excluding police; and (g) more than 12 hours duration.
[2] Characterized by: Any three of elements (a)—(d) described in footnote 1; duration of more than three hours; and more than 150 persons involved, exclusive of police.
[3] Involved usually no more than 150 persons but more than 5; lasted less than three hours; and was accomplished by any one or more of the following: vandalism, arson, looting or gunfire, and use of outside police or troops.

[a] As of 1971 "minor disturbances" were no longer included; total reflects the deletion of this statistic.

[x] Statistics not available.

Source: *Statistical Abstract of the United States, 1971,* and *Statistical Abstract of the United States, 1972.*

Table 4.2. Civil Disturbances and Related Deaths, 1968 to 1972,
by Season of the Year

Period	Total	Major [1]	Disturbances Serious [2]	Minor [3]	Related deaths
1968	435	26	54	355	83
January-March	43	2	4	37	9
April-June	179	19	27	133	52
July-September	159	5	20	134	21
October-December ..	54	0	3	51	1
1969	245	8	49	188	19
January-March	33	0	5	28	0
April-June	99	5	22	72	8
July-September	83	3	16	64	9
October-December ..	30	0	6	24	2
1970	195	18	58	119	33
January-March	45	8	18	19	10
April-June	65	7	17	41	11
July-September	60	3	17	40	6
October-December ..	25	0	6	19	6
1971	39 [a]	10	29	x	10
January-March	12 [a]	4	8	x	6
April-June	21 [a]	5	16	x	4
July-September	5 [a]	0	5	x	0
October-December ..	1 [a]	1	0	x	0
1972					
January-March	3	0	3	x	5

[1] Characterized by all of the following: (a) vandalism; (b) arson; (c) looting or gunfire; (d) outside police forces or troops used; (e) curfew imposed; (f) more than 300 people involved, excluding police; and (g) more than 12 hours duration.

[2] Characterized by: Any three of elements (a)—(d) described in footnote 1; duration of more than three hours; and more than 150 persons involved, exclusive of police.

[3] Involved usually no more than 150 persons but more than 5; lasted less than three hours; and was accomplished by any one or more of the following: vandalism, arson, looting or gunfire, and use of outside police or troops.

[a] As of 1971 "minor disturbances" were no longer included; total reflects the deletion of this statistic.

[x] Statistics not available.

Source: *Statistical Abstract of the United States, 1971*, and *Statistical Abstract of the United States, 1972*.

Two of the most highly publicized and widely known examples of civil disturbances are the 1967 riots, particularly those in Newark, New Jersey, and Detroit, Michigan, and the 1968 disruptions in Chicago, Illinois, during the Democratic National

Convention. These incidents received extensive treatment from the news media and prompted the national government to appoint groups of distinguished citizens to investigate both the nature and the causes of these disruptions.

Asked to probe the 1967 disturbances, the Kerner Commission found that they were unable to identify a "typical" riot or a nationwide conspiracy behind these disorders. The commission members found them to be rooted in local conditions. Racial in character, the civil disorders were directed against symbols of white America—white authority and white property—rather than against specific white persons. Interpreted as actions signifying black demands for fuller participation in and a greater material share of American society, commission members pointed to the severely disadvantaged conditions of many blacks, to local government unresponsive to these conditions, and to federal programs inadequate to effect significant changes in these conditions. Conditions of this nature in the ghetto produced deep and pervasive grievances and frustrations which, when coupled with a series of more immediate, tension-heightening incidents, permitted a further incident, frequently routine or trivial, to become the breaking point which led to the outbreaks of violence.

The group appointed to investigate the disturbances in Chicago during the Democratic National Convention released their findings in a controversial report entitled *Rights in Conflict* prepared by the study group's director, Daniel Walker. The so-called Walker Report pointed to the differences between the Chicago disturbances and the riots of 1967.

> Unlike other recent big city riots, including those in Chicago itself, the events of convention week did not consist of looting and burning, followed by mass arrests. To a shocking extent they consisted of crowd-police battles in the parks as well as the streets. And the shock was intensified by the presence in the crowds (which included some anarchists and revolutionaries) of large numbers of innocent dissenting citizens.

The disturbances in Chicago were not racial but primarily political; the study group considered them a classic confrontation between the rights of dissenters and the right of a city or state to protect its citizens and its property. This controversial report, a report which the United States Government Printing Office refused to print because of the obscenities contained in the document, assigned major responsibility for the violence that erupted to city officials and the police force, suggesting that what occurred may have been a "police riot."

These two, the 1967 riots and the 1968 incidents in Chicago, are illustrative of the complex relationship that exists between protest and group violence. Addressing itself to this relationship, the Skolnick Commission found that most incidents of protest in contemporary America are not only *not* violent, but that when violence does occur, authorities bear a major responsibility. The commission has stated:

> . . . the results of our research suggest that mass protest is a outgrowth of social, economic and political conditions; that such violence as occurs is usually not planned, but arises out of an *interaction* between protesters and the reaction of authorities; and that recommendations concerning the prevention of violence which do not address the issue of fundamental social, economic and political change are fated to be largely irrelevant and frequently self-defeating.

A final point about violence should be considered. While the term "violence" is frequently used, it does not lend itself to a clear, precise, and universally accepted definition. For example, the Skolnick Commission noted:

> The term "violence" is frequently employed to discredit forms of behavior considered improper, reprehensible, or threatening by specific groups which, in turn, may mask their own violent response with the rhetoric of order or progress.

The Reverend William Sloane Coffin has contended that exploitation is the essence of violence. By his definition, racism, poverty, hunger, the absence of adequate medical care, unemployment—all of which exist in varying degrees in the United States—are examples of societal, or institutional, violence.

While this definition is not widely recognized, most Americans would subscribe to the Skolnick Commission definition: "violence is the intentional use of force to injure, to kill, or destroy property." Yet even if one accepts such a definition, not all acts covered by it would be seen as acts that should be universally condemned. Muhammed Ali earns his living by violence in the boxing ring, a sport society finds to be quite legitimate. If he were to do the same thing on the street, he would be put into jail and condemned by society. History books praise the participants in the Boston Tea Party and term the English laws passed in reaction to the incident the "Intolerable Acts." But these history books may very likely condemn the action of the Berrigan brothers at Catonsville and term the government's reaction to that incident the proper administration of law and order. Many find reprehensible the death of a university student as the result of the bombing of a university building used for war-related research, but the death of a university student as the result of bullets fired by National Guardsmen or state police is considered justifiable. According to the Skolnick report, "Violence . . . is prescribed or condoned through political processes and decisions. The violence of the warrior in the service of the state is applauded; that of the rebel or insurgent against the state condemned."

It is clear that any discussion of violence is conditioned to a great extent by one's relationship to society. Its political nature must be understood. Thus with respect to the relationship between violence and mass protest the Skolnick Commission concluded:

> *Almost uniformly, the participants in mass protest today see their grievances as rooted in the existing arrangements of power and authority in contemporary society, and they view their own activity as political action—on a direct or symbolic level—aimed at altering those arrangements.* A common theme, from the ghetto to the university, is the rejection of dependency and external control, a staking of new boundaries, and a demand for significant control over events within those boundaries. This theme is far from new in American history. There have been violent clashes over institutional control in this country from its beginnings.

In its essence, dissent consists of one's disagreement with certain ideas, practices, and/or forms. By its very nature, dissent can be, and often is, a complex, bewildering, unpopular phenomenon. Frequently dissent is that of a minority seeking redress of grievances from a majority. Confronted by an unsympathetic majority, the dissenter sees his task as one of educating the majority, making the majority aware of the justness of his cause, and persuading them to respond to his grievances in a positive way. It is not only the nature of the grievance that is to be taken into consideration, however. The means used by the dissenter to educate and seek redress must also be considered. Both the content and the means of protest are of significance.

In recent years a large outpouring of dissent and protest has occurred in a wide variety of forms, from the casting of ballots and the holding of rallies, to the use of sit-ins, boycotts, and other kinds of nonviolent civil disobedience, to the bombings of public buildings, and the assassination of public officials. These divergent forms, which have been loudly praised and vigorously condemned in a variety of social circles, have stimulated a national dialogue and debate on what can be termed the "ethics of dissent," a dialogue that has yet to be ended and a debate that has yet to be resolved.

Chapter 5

Is Contemporary

Dissent Justified?

Consisting of a series of separate articles, this chapter presents a variety of perspectives on current dissent and protest in the United States. Primarily addressing themselves to the question of whether contemporary dissent is justified or not, these articles raise penetrating and provocative questions about both the nature of society and the nature of dissent.

"Points of Rebellion," William O. Douglas

United States Supreme Court Justice William O. Douglas provides a broad overview of the reasons for dissent in contemporary America. In this article, based on his book by the same title, Justice Douglas suggests the need for a vast restructuring of American society and implies a future of heightened protest activities. With which "points" do you find yourself in agreement with Justice Douglas and with which "points" do you find yourself in disagreement? If you took him at his word, what characteristics would a newly structured society have to possess?

A 16-year-old boy in Tokyo is symbolic of the dissent that is sweeping Japan. Japan has become identified with U.S. militarism, and some say Japan is now thoroughly subdued by the U.S. military approach to world problems. Japan is a huge U.S.

Originally appeared in *Playboy* magazine; copyright © 1969 by Justice William O. Douglas. Reprinted by permission of Robert Lantz-Candida Donadio Literary Agency, Inc.

Air Force base. It is also the only means by which the Seventh Fleet replenishes its supplies and is able to continue its operations in Far Eastern waters.

What worries the 16-year-old from Tokyo? The U.S. fear of Peking is the only major reason for our conversion of Japan into a military base. Yet neither the youth of Japan nor the older generation fears China. "We are blood brothers and have lived side by side for centuries."

Why, then, does Japan tolerate U.S. military bases in her country? The answer is an overwhelming fear of Russia.

That fear of the Japanese is as senseless as our own fear of Peking. Each senseless fear feeds the other. Whatever the Japanese youth may think of Russia, he sees the American military presence in Japan as inexorably involving Japan in a conflict with Peking. Our presence there has already had dire consequences, from the Japanese international viewpoint. They were pressured by us into recognizing Taipeh, a step that many Japanese—young and old—deem morally wrong. For the real China is mainland China, with 800,000,000 people. Peking, not Taipeh, is the mirror of the 21st Century, with all of its troublesome problems. The Japanese—especially the young—want to get on with those problems, so that they will not fester and worsen.

The youthful dissenter in the U.S. probably does not see the Asian situation as clearly as the Japanese dissenter, unless he gets to Vietnam or nearby. Yet more and more of the youth of America are instinctively horrified at the way Johnson avoided all constitutional procedures and slyly maneuvered us into an Asian war. There was no national debate over a declaration of war. The lies and half-truths they were told and the phony excuses advanced gradually made most Americans dubious of the integrity of our leadership.

Moreover, the lack of any apparent threat to American interests, whether Vietnam was fascist, Communist, or governed in the ancient Chinese mandarin tradition (as it was for years), compounded the American doubts concerning our Vietnam venture. And the youth rebelled violently when Johnson used his long arm to try to get colleges to discipline the dissenters and when he turned the Selective Service System into a vindictive weapon for use against the protesters.

Various aspects of militarism have produced kindred protests among the youth both here and in Japan. There is, I believe, a common suspicion among youth around the world that the design for living, fashioned for them by their politically bankrupt elders, destines them either to the nuclear incinerator or to a life filled with a constant fear of it.

The Japanese say that the most dreadful time in history was the period when only one nation (the U.S.) had the atomic bomb. Then that bomb was used, and Hiroshima is not forgotten. To the Japanese, a sense of security came when Russia acquired the same bomb. They reason that that created a deterrent to the use of nuclear force by any of the great powers.

But we know that preparedness and the armament race inevitably lead to war. Thus it ever has been and ever will be. Armaments are no more of a deterrent to war than the death sentence is to murder. We know from our own experience that among felonies, the incidence of murder is no higher in Michigan and Minnesota (where the death penalty was abolished years ago) than in California and New York. Moreover, when Delaware restored the death penalty eight years ago, there was an increase, not a decrease, in the rate of homicides.

If the war that comes is a nuclear conflict, the end of planetary life is probable. If it is a war with conventional weapons, bankruptcy is inevitable. Modern technological war is much too expensive to fight. Vietnam has bled our country at a rate of two and a half billion dollars a month.

We still have the Pentagon, with a fantastic budget that enables it to dream of putting down the much-needed revolutions that will arrive in Peru, in the Philippines and in other benighted countries. Where is the force that will restrain the Pentagon? Would a President dare face it down?

The strength of a center of power such as the Pentagon is measured in part by the billions of dollars it commands. Its budget is greater than the total Federal budget in 1957. Beyond that is the self-perpetuating character of the Pentagon. Its officer elite is, of course, subject to some controls, but those controls are mostly formal.

It has a magnetism and an energy of its own. It exercises, moreover, a powerful impact on the public mind. Its public representatives are numerous and a phone call or a personal visit propels the spokesman into action. It has on the Hill one public-relations man for every two or three Congressmen and Senators. The mass media—essentially the voice of the establishment—reflect mostly the mood of the Pentagon and the causes the military-industrial complex espouses. So we, the people, are relentlessly pushed in the direction that the Pentagon desires.

The push in that direction is increased by powerful foreign interests. The China lobby, financed by the millions of dollars extorted and extracted from America by the Kuomintang, uses vast sums to brainwash us about Asia. The Shah of Iran hires Madison Avenue houses to give a democratic luster to his military, repressive dictatorship. And so it goes.

I have, perhaps, put into sophisticated words the worries and concerns of modern youth. Their wisdom is often instinctive, or they may acquire a revealing insight from a gross statement made by their elders. But part of their overwhelming fear is the prospect of the military regime that has ruled us since Truman and the ominous threat that the picture holds. Is it our destiny to kill Russians? To kill Chinese? Why can't we work at cooperative schemes and search for the common ground binding all mankind together?

We seem to be going in the other direction. This year, we will spend $891,500,000 for developing the ABM, which is almost as much as we will allocate to community-action and model-cities programs combined; we will spend 1.7 billion dollars on new Navy ships, which is close to what we will spend on education for the poor; we will spend 8 billion dollars on new-weapons research, which is more than the current cost of the Medicare program; and so on and so on.

Race is another source of dissent. Negroes want parity as respects human dignity—parity as respects equal justice and parity in economic opportunities.

Police practices are anti-Negro. Unemployment is anti-Negro. Education is anti-Negro.

Almost 50 percent of the Negroes live in a state of poverty. Over half of the 6,500,000 Americans of Mexican descent in the Southwest also live in poverty. Our food program is another cause of dissent. Millions upon millions of dollars go to corporate and other farmers to restrict production and to guarantee profits for the producers. Only meager amounts are made available to the poor.

Thus, in one year, Texas producers (who constitute .02 percent of the Texas population) received $250,000,000 in subsidies, while the Texas poor (who constitute 28.8 percent of the Texas population) received $7,500,000 in food assistance.

Of the 30,000,000 poor at the national level, fewer than 6,000,000 participate in either the food-stamp program or the surplus-commodities program.

Bias in the laws against the poor is another source of dissent. Vagrancy laws are one example. Many cities make being poor a crime. A man who wanders, looking for a job, is suspect, and he and his kind are arrested by the thousands each year. The police use vagrancy as an excuse for arresting people on suspicion—a wholly unconstitutional procedure in our country.

Bias against the poor is present in the usury laws and in the practices of consumer credit. There are some credit transactions where the monthly payment is so restricted and the accumulation of interest so rapid that one who makes time payments for ten years will owe more at the end than at the beginning. For the poor, the interest rates often rise to 1000 percent a year.

We got rid of our debtors' prisons in the last century. But today's garnishment proceedings are as destructive and as vicious as the debtors' dungeons. Employers have commonly discharged workers whose wages are garnisheed, and the total runs over 250,000 a year. In many states, the percentage of wages garnisheed has been so high that a family is often reduced to a starvation level.

Congress in 1968 passed a law requiring full disclosure of all consumer-credit charges. It also banned the discharge of employees whose wages are garnisheed and it reduced the percentage of the weekly wage that may be garnisheed.

But the charges for consumer credit are governed almost entirely by state law; and in 1969, practically all the states (at least 48) were asked to adopt a so-called model code, fashioned by the finance-company lobby, that increases permissible charges and makes the hold of the lender even tighter on the poor. Needless to say, the finance-company lobby did not recommend the introduction of neighborhood credit unions, whose interest is low.

Landlord-tenant laws are also filled with bias against the poor. They have been written by the landlords' lobby, making the tenant's duty to pay rent absolute and the landlord's duty to make repairs practically nonexistent.

Disemployment due to technological advances is becoming endemic. Private industry will not be able to take care of the employment needs of our mounting population. Yet no public sector of consequence is provided. Only the welfare system is offered and in the eyes of the poor, it pays the poor to be poor.

Another main source of disaffection among our youth stems from the reckless way in which the establishment has despoiled the earth. The matter was put recently by a 16-year-old boy, who asked his father, "Why did you let me be born?" His father, taken aback, asked the reason for the silly question. The question turned out to be relevant.

At the present rate of the use of oxygen in the air, it may not be long before there is not enough for people to breathe. The percentage of carbon dioxide in some areas is already dangerously high. Sunshine and green leaves may not be able to make up the growing deficiency of oxygen that exists only in a thin belt around the earth.

Everyone knows—including the youthful dissenters—that Lake Erie is now only a tub filled with stinking sewage and wastes. Many of our rivers are open sewers. Our estuaries—essential breeding grounds for marine life—are fast being either destroyed by construction projects or poisoned by pollution. The virgin stands of timber are virtually gone. Only remnants of the once-immortal redwoods remain. Pesticides have killed millions of birds, putting some of them in line for extinction. Hundreds of trout streams have been destroyed by highway engineers and their faulty plans. The wilderness disappears each year under the ravages of bulldozers, highway builders and men in search of metals that will make them rich. Our coast lines are being ruined by men who look for oil yet have not mastered the technology enough to know how to protect the public interest in the process.

The youthful dissenters are not experts in these matters. But when they see all the wonders of nature being ruined, they ask, "What natural law gives the establishment the right to ruin the rivers, the lakes, the oceans, the beaches and even the air?" And if one tells them that the important thing is making money and increasing the G.N.P., they turn away in disgust.

Their protest is not only against what the establishment is doing to the earth but against the callous attitude of those who claim the God-given right to wreak that damage on the nation without rectifying the wrong.

There have always been grievances and youth has been the agitator. Why, then, is today different? Why does dissent loom so ominously?

At the consumer-credit level and at the level of housing, the deceptive practices of the establishment have multiplied. Beyond that is the factor of communication, which, in the field of consumer credit, implicates more and more people who, no matter how poor, with all their beings want the merchandise on display.

Beyond all that is another, more basic reason. Political action today is most difficult, for the major parties are controlled by the establishment and the result is a form of political bankruptcy.

A letter to me from an American GI in Vietnam written in early 1969 states that bald truth:

Somewhere in our history—though not intentionally—we slowly moved from a government of a chosen few—that either by birth, family tradition or social standing, a minority possessing all the wealth and power now in turn control the destiny of mankind.

This GI ends by saying, "You see, Mr. Douglas, the greatest cause of alienation is that my generation has no one to turn to." And he adds,

With all the hatred and violence that exist throughout the world, it is that someone, regardless of personal risk, must stand up and represent the feelings, the hopes, the dreams and desires of the hundreds of thousands of Americans who died, are dying and will die in search of truth.

This young man, as a result of his experiences in the crucible of Vietnam and in the riots at home, has decided to enter politics and run for office as spokesman for the poor and underprivileged of our nation.

Political action that will recast the balance will take years. Meanwhile, an overwhelming sense of futility possesses the younger generation. How can any pressing, needed reforms or changes or reversals be achieved? There is, in the end, a feeling that the individual is caught in a pot of glue and is utterly helpless.

The truth is that a vast bureaucracy now runs the country, irrespective of the party in power. The decision to spray sagebrush or mesquite trees in order to increase the production of grass and make a cattle baron richer is that of a faceless person in some Federal agency. Those who prefer horned owls or coyotes do not even have a chance to be heard.

How does one fight an entrenched farm lobby or an entrenched highway lobby? How does one get even a thin slice of the farm benefits, which go to the rich, into the lunch boxes of the poor?

How does one give HEW and its state counterparts a humane approach and rob the bureaucrats of a desire to discriminate against an illegitimate child or to conduct midnight raids without the warrants needed before even a poor man's home may be entered by the police?

Most of the questions are out of reach of any remedy for the average person. The truth is that a vast restructuring of our society is needed if remedies are to become available to the average person. Without that restructuring, the good will that holds society together will be slowly dissipated.

It is that sense of futility that permeates the present series of protests and dissents. Where there is a sense of futility and it persists, there is violence; and that is where we are today.

"Cause for Protest?," David T. Naylor

Providing statistics that compare the status and relationship of white Americans to nonwhite Americans, the author asks the reader to draw his own conclusions, based on an examination of the data presented, in regard to the nature of contemporary society and the future of dissent and protest in this country.

Black protest is not a recent phenomenon for it has deep roots in American history, roots that extend over several hundreds of years. During that period of time various alternatives have been proposed, various individuals have provided direction, and various methods have been employed. Yet despite the efforts of such leaders as Frederick Douglas, W. E. B. DuBois, Booker T. Washington, Marcus Garvey, and Dr. Martin Luther King, Jr., to name but a few from a long distinguished list, black protest continues as one of the main characteristics of contemporary American life.

Since the beginnings of the modern "Negro revolt" in the 1950s, Americans have become increasingly conscious, perhaps more than ever, of the nature and extent of black protest. Some gains have been made—the Supreme Court has ruled *de jure* (of law) segregation unconstitutional and ordered the end of segregated schools, Congress has passed the 1964 Civil Rights Law, the 1965 Voting Rights Law, and the 1968 Open Housing Law, and an American President has vowed, "We shall overcome!" In addition, various institutions—business, educational, religious, military, etc.—have openly acknowledged racist practices and announced programs to eliminate them.

To a number of Americans, these and other similar events in recent years signified progress and much contemporary discussion centers around an assessment of that progress. Despite a myriad of books and articles that have appeared in recent years on this topic, an accurate assessment of the significance of recent events is difficult to obtain, for many works clearly reflect the philosophies and biases of their authors.

One approach to this subject which may be of value is to consult statistics compiled by a relatively neutral source which compare the relative position of white and nonwhite—principally black—citizens. Such information may be helpful in ascertaining both the past and the present status of each group and in assessing the significance of the events of recent years.

As you peruse the following data, what conclusions can you draw? If you find disparities between the two groups, what explanations can you offer? Is it possible to determine whether the lot of nonwhite citizens has improved in recent years? Why or why not?

Table 5.1 provides information with respect to the life expectancy of an American at birth. Who seems to live the longest in the United States, males or females? How do you account for this? What differences emerge in a comparison of the life expectancy of whites with that of nonwhites? Why does white-male life expectancy seem to be identical to black-female life expectancy? Using these and similar comparisons, do you discern any trends in the fifty-year period of time covered in Table 5.1?

Table 5.1. Expectation of Life at Birth: 1920 to 1970 (In number of years)

YEAR	Total	White Male	Female	Total	Negro and Other Male	Female
1920	54.9	54.4	55.6	45.3	45.5	45.2
1930	61.4	59.7	63.5	48.1	47.3	49.2
1940	64.2	62.1	66.6	53.1	51.1	54.9
1950	69.1	66.5	72.2	60.8	59.1	62.9
1955	70.5	67.4	73.7	63.7	61.4	66.1
1960	70.6	67.4	74.1	63.6	61.1	66.3
1965	71.0	67.6	74.7	64.1	61.1	67.4
1968	71.1	67.5	74.9	63.7	60.1	67.5
1970 (prel.)	71.7	68.1	75.4	64.6	60.5	68.9

Source: *Statistical Abstract of the United States, 1972.*

Table 5.2 is concerned with infant and maternal deaths, providing data over a thirty-year period of time. Do differences between the rates for whites and the rates for nonwhites appear for either or both of these types of deaths? What factors influence these rates?

Table 5.2. Infant and Maternal Death Rates, by Race—1940 to 1970
(Deaths per 1,000 live births)

ITEM	1940	1950	1955	1960	1965	1968	1970 (prel.)
Infant deaths [1]	47.0	29.2	26.4	26.0	24.7	21.8	19.8
White	43.2	26.8	23.6	22.9	21.5	19.2	(NA)
Negro and Other	73.8	44.5	42.8	43.2	40.3	34.5	(NA)
Maternal deaths [2]	376.0	83.3	47.0	37.1	31.6	24.5	24.7
White	319.8	61.1	32.8	26.0	21.0	16.6	(NA)
Negro and Other	773.5	221.6	130.3	97.9	83.7	63.6	(NA)

[1] Represents deaths of infants under one year of age, exclusive of fetal deaths.
[2] Per 100,000 live births from deliveries and complications of pregnancy, childbirth, and the puerperium.

NA—Not Available.

Source: *Statistical Abstract of the United States, 1972.*

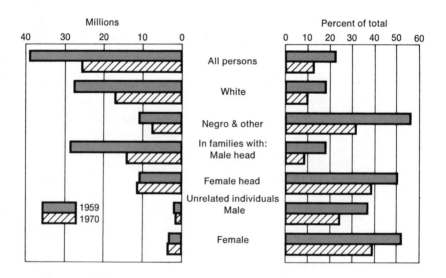

Fig. 5.1. Persons in Families and Unrelated Individuals below Low Income Level, by Sex of Head, for 1959 and 1970.

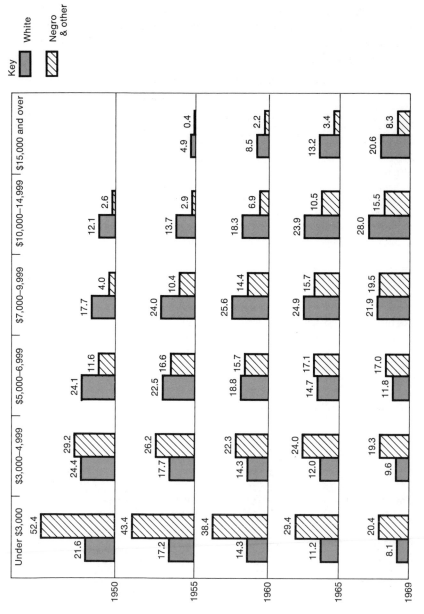

Fig. 5.2. Money Income—Percent Distribution of Families by Income Level and Race in Constant (1969) Dollars.

Both Figs. 5.1 and 5.2 deal with the money income of families. Figure 5.1 provides data with respect to persons or families below the low-income or poverty level. What conclusions can you draw from an examination of this information?

One's position in American society is to a great extent conditioned by his or her income. Figure 5.2 shows the percent distribution of white and nonwhite families by income level. How do you account for the differences that appear between these two groups? Table 5.3 compares the median incomes of black and white families and the ratio between them. Over a period of nine years, what trend emerges, if any? How do you explain this?

Table 5.3. Median Family Income—Ratio of Black and White Families, 1964–1972

Year	Black Family Median Income	White Family Median Income	Ratio of Black Income to White Income
1964	$ 3,724	$ 6,858	.50
1965	$ 3,886	$ 7,251	.50
1966	$ 4,507	$ 7,792	.58
1967	$ 4,875	$ 8,234	.59
1968	$ 5,360	$ 8,937	.60
1969	$ 5,999	$ 9,794	.61
1970	$ 6,279	$10,236	.61
1971	$ 6,440	$10,672	.60
1972	$ 6,864	$11,549	.59

Source: *Bureau of the Census.*

Table 5.4. Median Income of Families with Heads 25 Years Old and Over by Years of School Completed and Race of Family Head, 1961 and 1970

Years of School Completed	1961 White Median	1961 Nonwhite Median	1970 White Median	1970 Nonwhite Median
Elementary School	$4,419	$2,593	$ 6,933	$ 4,930
High School	$6,344	$4,115	$10,579	$ 7,492
1 to 3 years	$6,036	$3,711	$ 9,509	$ 6,563
4 years	$6,548	$4,773	$11,054	$ 8,239
College	$8,560	$6,593	$14,127	$11,573
1 to 3 years	$7,586	$ *	$12,487	$ 9,968
4 years	$9,503	$ *	$15,841	$14,470

* Too few for the purpose of tabulation.

Source: *Statistical Abstract of the United States, 1972.*

Many people frequently link educational attainment with income level and suggest that a positive relationship—the higher one is, the higher the other will be—exists between the two. Is this relationship supported by the figures contained in Table 5.4? Does this relationship hold for both groups? Why is it that on the average a white citizen with less education than a nonwhite citizen will earn as much or more? For example, a white with only an elementary-school education will earn more than a nonwhite citizen who has been to high school from one to three years and almost as much as a nonwhite citizen who has graduated from high school. How do you explain these figures?

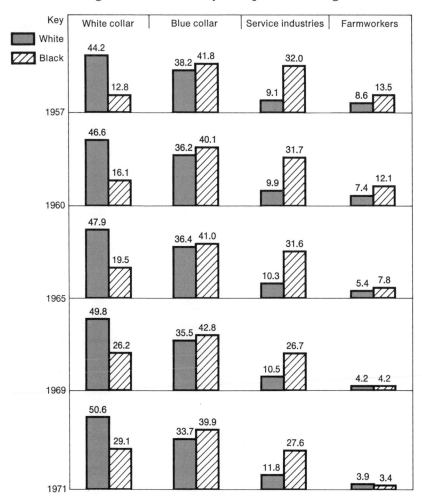

Fig. 5.3. Employed Persons, by Occupation and Race, from 1957 to 1971.

An important determinant of one's social status, life-style, and outlook is the type of job that he or she holds. Figure 5.3 distinguishes four occupational types and gives a percent distribution by race in those four occupational types. What type of jobs do *most* white citizens seem to hold? What types of jobs would be included in this category? What types of jobs do *most* nonwhite citizens seem to hold? What types of jobs would be included in this category? What reasons can you give for the difference? As you survey the period of time covered in Fig. 5.3, what trends are apparent? How do you interpret this?

One of the most serious problems to plague industrial societies is that of unemployment. Figure 5.4 provides a comparison of the unemployment rate for both white and nonwhite citizens overall and in selected areas. How do you account for these disparities? What does this suggest to you about problems that arise in various areas of the country?

Some will no doubt find these statistics shocking while others will see them as mere reflections of "the natural order of things." In the influential book, *Black Power: The Politics of Liberation in America,* authors Stokely Carmichael and Charles Hamilton suggested that statistics of this nature reflect the basic racist character of American society. They contended that two forms of racism exist, one being individual racism and the other institutional racism. Individual racism was described as consisting of overt acts taken against people of another race for the purpose of doing them harm. Institutional racism, a more subtle and virulent strain, was seen as consisting of covert acts which subjugate a racial group. Operating within the established and respected forces of the society,

> it has perpetuated a vicious circle—the poverty cycle—in which the black communities are denied good jobs, and therefore stuck with a low income and therefore unable to obtain a good education with which to obtain jobs. They cannot qualify for credit at most reputable places; they then resort to unethical merchants who take advantage of them by charging high prices for inferior goods. They end up having less funds to buy in bulk, thus unable to reduce overall costs. They remain trapped.

The authors added:

> . . . The society does nothing meaningful about institutional racism because the black community has been the

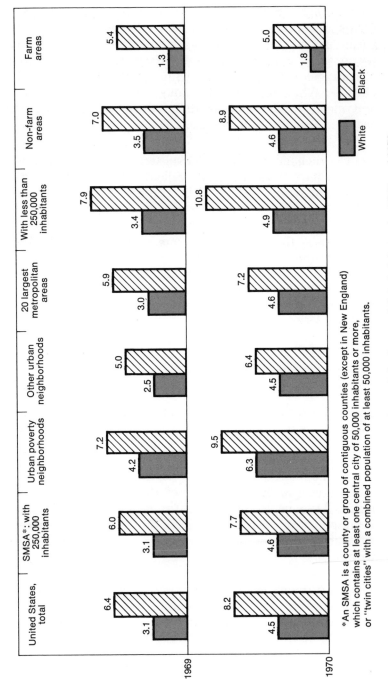

Fig. 5.4. Percentage of Unemployment, by Race and Selected Areas, for 1969 and 1970.

*An SMSA is a county or group of contiguous counties (except in New England) which contains at least one central city of 50,000 inhabitants or more, or "twin cities" with a combined population of at least 50,000 inhabitants.

creation of, and dominated by a combination of oppressive forces and special interests in the white community. . . . Institutional racism has been maintained deliberately by the power structure and through indifference, inertia and lack of courage on the part of the white masses as well as petty officials. Whenever black demands for change become loud and clear, indifference is replaced by active opposition based on fear and self-interest.

Are Carmichael and Hamilton substantially correct in their analysis? Do these statistics really reflect forms of institutional racism in American society? What other explanations are possible?

Does a survey of both the absolute and relative trends in this data suggest that the plight of nonwhite Americans is improving, remaining stationary, or regressing? In your opinion, based on this and similar data, should the pace of black protest accelerate or decelerate? What implications are suggested for both the immediate and long-range future of America? Is there cause for protest?

"Dear Brats," Tom Anderson

A powerful dissent to the student protest movement, this article by Tom Anderson suggests that contemporary student protest is but the product of hypocritical "spoiled, deluded and brainwashed brats." Contained in his condemnation of student protesters is a strong defense of the American status quo. A comparison of this article with that by Justice Douglas is instructive for it reveals the different assumptions of each about the nature of man, the nature of society, and consequently the nature of contemporary dissent.

It is my annual custom at this time of year to write an inspiring message to America's militant youth. Since I always strive to make these messages sincere and "from the heart," I shall do my thing this year with that uppermost in mind:

"Dear Brats" by Tom Anderson first appeared in the June 1969 issue of *American Opinion* (Belmont, Massachusetts 02178) and is reprinted by permission of the publisher.

Dear spoiled, deluded, and brainwashed brats:

I am sick of you. I am sick of your professors, your administrators, your clergymen (if any), your parents, and others who have come very close to ruining an entire generation of young Americans.

The agnostic pragmatists who call themselves "Liberals" have taught you: (1) that there are no clear distinctions between right and wrong; (2) that there are no eternal verities, no absolute truths; (3) that environment determines truth and, since environment constantly changes, everything is relative; (4) that "life adjustment," not inculcation of principles and disciplines, is the aim of education; (5) that patriotism is absurd and out of date; and (6) that the government owes you a drink of some magic elixir called equality and a "decent" standard of living. The frauds further proclaim that you are not responsible for what you have become; that "Man is the product of his hereditary environment and you cannot expect him to rise above it." I doubt that many of you will.

You young militants, apparently brought up on the permissive nonreality of Dr. Spock, insist on running away from reality. You bemoan the world you "never made." What you fail to understand is that you must live in the world as it is and as it can be. My prayer for you is this: "Lord, give them the courage to change the things they can change, to accept those they cannot change, and—above all—the wisdom to know the difference."

Some things we can and should change, and some we can't and shouldn't. You can raise a pig in your parlor all right. But, it won't change the pig—only your parlor. So be *for* change as long as it's change for the better, recognizing that ruts are just graves with the ends removed.

Yet why change just to be changing? Why *destroy* the American system which has produced the highest standard of living in human history, just because that system is not perfect? Our Republic, with its capitalist economy, is indeed imperfect—but it is the least reprehensible system of government and economics which exists. There will never be a perfect system until there are perfect people; there will never be perfect people this side of Heaven. No society is better than the *individuals* in it. No nation advances except as the citizens who comprise it grow as individuals.

The collectivists, so-called "Liberals," seem to have convinced you that a socialist government can legislate unsuccessful people into prosperity by legislating successful people out of it. If that is true, why should a man work to succeed? The fact is that there is no such thing as equality. We cannot be free *and* equal. Free men are not equal and equal men are not free. While all men are created equal in the eyes of God and the law, they don't long stay equal even there. God penalizes unrepentant sinners, and the law penalizes repeating criminals.

So you want to replace "dog eat dog" with "dog love dog"? Both are animalism, and can only return civilization to the jungle.

Oh, I know you are constantly hearing that we must have equality not only here but with the rest of the world if we are to live in a peaceful socialist One World with our brothers. . . . The fact is that all mature men and women, all mature nations, are *inherently* unequal. That's why materialist America, with only six percent of the world's people and seven percent of the world's land, produces half of the world's goods. The sinister, selfish, and square American System of Free Enterprise (our profit and loss system) has enabled Americans to own seventy-one percent of the world's cars, fifty-six percent of its telephones, eighty-three percent of its TV sets, and (forgive me, hippies) ninety percent of its bathtubs.

The inventiveness of the American system has long been the envy of the world. The only new thing the Yippie Set has produced is a new drug mixing LSD and The Pill, so they can take a trip without the kids.

Meanwhile the voice from the Campus cries "hypocrisy!" at the community elders and the "Establishment." Students decry the "rat race," the "crushing materialism," our "money-mad society"—and then wire home, collect, for $200 to finance a spring bash of booze and sex at Fort Lauderdale, or a trip to New York for a parade to honor the Vietcong.

If you students want to rebel against "hypocrisy," why don't you rebel against an educational system whose "Liberal" teachers give you low marks unless you repeat their Leftist fairy tales at examination time?

If "hypocrisy" really offends you, why don't you rebel against the "Christian" heads of your Divinity Schools who are so quick to proclaim that they don't even believe in the divinity and resurrection of Christ?

If you want to rebel against the War in Vietnam, why don't you ask why our military is not being allowed to defeat a little country smaller than the state of Missouri?

If you want to rebel against the faceless, impersonal, giant corporations, why don't you demand to know why so many of them are trading with the arsenal of an enemy killing our soldiers in the field?

If you are opposed to materialism, if your heart bleeds for the disadvantaged, you guilt-ridden phonies should know that, just to help you defeat hypocrisy, you may turn over to me your new car, TV, stereo, tape-recorder, electric blanket, hair drier, camera, or fancy "mod" wardrobe, and I will personally see that they are distributed among the poor. Why don't you "idealists" practice what you preach?

Why don't you rebel against a rigged communications system which is brainwashing the American people? Not so? How long since you've seen an anti-Communist TV program or movie? Ever? Communism is the scourge of the world, yet you either ignore it or embrace it. It is the cause of most of the world's problems today, but you are almost never told the truth about it—not by your professors, movies, television, magazines, or newspapers. Why not, kids? Think about it a minute.

I don't blame you for being upset by the Establishment. You've been *had* by the Establishment. But the Establishment is *not* capitalism and the system of individual enterprise. Nor even what was formerly known as "Americanism." It is a combination of industrial cartelists, education and foundation bureaucrats, Leftist churchmen, and lightweight communicators who are deliberately trying to convert this nation into a Marxist-Fascist welfare state for their own aggrandizement and convenience. Most of these people are neither Marxists nor Fascists, but they are manipulated by Communists and are playing the Communist game. What is more, they are using *you* as pawns in that game.

Still, you never seem to learn.

One evening recently I spoke to a small crowd at Vanderbilt University. During the question and answer period, one sweet young thing with his hair on his shoulders stood and declared: "We're not Communists. We're anarchists. We don't want total government. We want no government. We believe in atheism, free love, and homosexuality between consenting adults."

How does a square like me "have dialogue" with that? I merely asked the shaven audience why they would sit there, inert, and let such slobs destroy their university, their country, and their freedom. No answer.

No, you never seem to learn.

If you "moderates," you uncommitted students, think that it is wrong and inexcusable to invite a self-proclaimed Marxist homosexual like Allen Ginsberg, a self-proclaimed criminal and anarchist like Eldridge Cleaver, or a head of the Young Communist League like Mike Zagarell, to speak on your campus, then why don't you do something about it?

People keep telling me that the campus anarchists, pacifists, Marxists, pot addicts, and "fairies" are a very small minority. Very well, maybe so. But tell me why an overwhelming majority of decent young people will sit by supinely while its universities are being hijacked and burned. More appealing than the outrages perpetrated by the collegiate punks, pinks, and perverts is the spineless acquiescence of the student majority.

We are constantly told that only two percent of you students are disrupting the campuses. But that is not true. The cowardly, apathetic, and silent ninety-eight percent of you who are *uncommitted* are guilty of letting it happen.

Most college students, according to a recent national survey, believe that the chief benefit of a college education is to increase one's earning power. Are these the same "idealists" who are bemoaning the cold commercial world they never made? Often they are. The point is that while money is not the main reason to go to college, neither is making over the world to suit the Marxist fairy tale.

Thousands of small businesses, such as the one I operate, couldn't care less whether employees went to college. The main reason to seek a higher education is to lift your horizon; to enable you to appreciate the finer things of life; to help you to make a good life, not a good living. When you graduate from college you are not educated. But you should have learned what it means to be educated; you should have the desire and the know-how to *get* an education. The first thing an educated person learns to do is walk alone. Why don't you try it sometime? Get out of the mob, kids. Learn to be your own man. That's what integrity is all about.

Oh, I know that this sounds like tough talk. We so-called Conservatives are prone to such intolerance. But, one of the greatest problems of this country is that tolerance has become so excessive as to amount to cowardly permissiveness. In my book, one is not capable of genuine tolerance unless he is capable of honest conviction—which means a commitment to intolerance for lies and sham and fraud and perversion. A person unable to arrive at convictions is a person morally immature.

When things are morally and legally wrong, you are right to rebel. But your rebellion must be moral, legal, and constructive, or else *you* are wrong. Students don't have a moral or legal right to "take over" a building. They are violating property rights and the rights of other students, and they should be routed out with tear gas, arrested, and given jail sentences. That's the way it is in the real world!

The first requirement and obligation of the institution of learning is to build character. "Free speech" and "search for truth" do not include the right to promote subversion, insurrection, anarchy, arson, murder, and treason. Nor does "academic freedom" include the right publicly to push drugs, free sex, and Communism. Communism and other such perversions are like rape—they are not moot questions. Communism is not just another ideology or a political Party, but a criminal conspiracy to enslave the world. Communists should no more be given a collegiate platform than murderers, dope pushers, or smut peddlers.

Discipline, order and character are the foundation of learning, not permissiveness, anarchy, and perversion. The main purpose of a school, in my opinion, should be to build and discipline character. Chancellors, administrators, and teachers devoid of character cannot, of course, build character. This is where our educational system has failed. This is the explanation for revolutionary anarchy on the campus. As historians Will and Ariel Durant have written:

> Violent revolutions do not so much redistribute wealth as destroy it. There may be a redivision of the land, but the natural inequality of men soon recreates an inequality of positions and privileges. The only real revolution is in the enlightenment of the mind and the improvement of character. The only real emancipation is individual, and the only real revolutionists are philosophers and saints.

Freedom without the discipline of character is an absurdity. "Freedom now!" sounds great, I suppose, to those of you who are wet behind the ears. But, the phrase you should be hearing is "Discipline now!" In a civilized society, freedom without discipline is impossible. Those who cannot discipline themselves cannot long be allowed to run free. People who cannot muster the discipline to govern themselves are destined to be disciplined by dictators. If the prevailing government is too decadent to do the job, then some other government, from outside or within, will replace it, by force if necessary. Thus individual violence is replaced by government violence. And freedom is replaced by slavery, as in Cuba, Mainland China, Czecho-Slovakia, Poland, Romania, Russia and elsewhere.

The campus revolution, if continued on its present course, will lead to an escalating revolution in the streets followed by dictatorship. And it will be a Communist dictatorship. The leadership of the "take-over generation" has been taken over by the Communists.

Your campus anarchists want a showdown—and they are going to get it. Millions of the taxpayers they consider milk cows are sick of paying for the destruction of their schools and their country. Millions of us are tired of the excess of tolerance become license, of trying to reason with unreason, of cant and Bolshevik clichés that were dated when your grandfather was in knickers. The academic leaders may be afraid of the militant young fascists and anarchists who are trying to turn our free Republic into a police state, but we the *people* are not.

"To the American People," The President's Commission on Campus Unrest

Appointed by President Nixon following incidents on the campus of Kent State University and other college and university campuses, the President's Commission on Campus Unrest was headed by former Pennsylvania Governor William Scranton. This excerpt from the Commission's report reflects their findings in the form of an open letter to the American people. After surveying the basic reasons behind contemporary dissent, Commission members felt it necessary to caution against two dangers they observed—the increasing tendency of protesters to become violent and the tendency of other Americans toward an increasing intolerance of dissent.

Campus protest has been focused on three major questions: racial injustice, war, and the university itself.

The first issue is the unfulfilled promise of full justice and dignity for Blacks and other minorities. Blacks, like many others of different races and ethnic origins, are demanding today that the pledges of the Declaration of Independence and the Emancipation Proclamation be fulfilled now. Full social justice and dignity—an end to racism in all its human, social, and cultural forms—is a central demand of today's students—black, brown, and white.

William W. Scranton, Chairman, *The Report of the President's Commission on Campus Unrest* (Washington, D.C.: United States Government Printing Office, 1970).

A great majority of students and a majority of their elders oppose the Indochina war. Many believe it entirely immoral. And if the war is wrong, students insist, then so are all policies and practices that support it, from the draft to military research, from ROTC to recruiting for defense industry. This opposition has led to an ever-widening wave of student protests.

The shortcomings of the American university are the third target of student protest. The goals, values, administration, and curriculum of the modern university have been sharply criticized by many students. Students complain that their studies are irrelevant to the social problems that concern them. They want to shape their own personal and common lives, but find the university restrictive. They seek a community of companions and scholars, but find an impersonal multiversity. And they denounce the university's relationship to the war and to discriminatory racial practices.

Behind the student protest on these issues and the crisis of violence to which they have contributed lies the more basic crisis of understanding.

Americans have never shared a single culture, a single philosophy, or a single religion. But in most periods of our history, we have shared many common values, common sympathies, and a common dedication to a system of government which protects our diversity.

We are now in grave danger of losing what is common among us through growing intolerance of opposing views on issues and of diversity itself.

A "new" culture is emerging primarily among students. Membership is often manifested by differences in dress and life style. Most of its members have high ideals and great fears. They stress the need for humanity, equality, and the sacredness of life. They fear that nuclear war will make them the last generation in history. They see their elders as entrapped by materialism and competition, and as prisoners of outdated social forms. They believe their own country has lost its sense of human purpose. They see the Indochina war as an onslaught by a technological giant upon the peasant people of a small, harmless, and backward nation. The war is seen as draining resources from the urgent needs of social and racial justice. They argue that we are the first nation with sufficient resources to create not only decent lives for some but a decent society for all, and that we are failing to do so. They feel they must remake America in its own image.

But among the members of this new student culture, there is a growing lack of tolerance, a growing insistence that their own views must govern, an impatience with the slow procedures of liberal democracy, a growing denial of the humanity and good will of those who urge patience and restraint, and particularly of those whose duty it is to enforce the law. A small number of students have turned to violence; an increasing number, no terrorists themselves, would not turn even arsonists and bombers over to law enforcement officials.

At the same time, many Americans have reacted to this emerging culture with an intolerance of their own. They reject not only that which is impatient, unrestrained, and intolerant in the new culture of the young, but even that which is good. Worse, they reject the individual members of the student culture themselves. Distinctive dress alone is enough to insult and abuse. Increasing numbers of citizens believe that students who dissent or protest—even those who protest peacefully—deserve to be treated harshly. Some even say that when dissenters are killed, they have brought death upon themselves. Less and less do students and the larger community seek to understand or respect the viewpoint and motivations of others.

If this trend continues, if this crisis of understanding endures, the very survival of the nation will be threatened. A nation driven to use the weapons of war upon its youth is a nation that has lost part of its future. A nation whose young have become intolerant of diversity, intolerant of the rest of its citizenry, and intolerant of all traditional values simply because they are traditional has no generation worthy or capable of assuming leadership in the years to come.

The Testimony of Linda Hager Morse

In the United States District Court
Northern District of Illinois, Eastern Division
United States of America v. David T. Dellinger,
et. al., 69 CR 180
Before Judge Hoffman and a Jury,
Tuesday, December 16, 1969
10:00 o'clock A.M., pp. 11207–11416.

The trial of the Chicago 7 (or Chicago 8 if one includes Bobby Seale) was the direct result of events that occurred in the city of Chicago, Illinois, during the week of the 1968

Democratic National Convention. The charge against the defendants was essentially that of conspiring to incite a riot and crossing state lines with the intent of inciting a riot. These charges stemmed from a violation to Public Law 90–284 passed by the United States Congress in the Spring of 1968.

Miss Morse was not a defendant but a witness for the defense. Her testimony is taken from the court transcript and, except in cases where motions, repetitive questions, or, at least for the purposes of this book, extraneous testimony were deleted, the following testimony is that which was given in the court.

Linda Hager Morse, called as a witness on behalf of the defendants, having been first duly sworn, was examined and testified as follows:

Direct Examination

By Mr. Kunstler [1]

Q: Would you, Miss Morse, state your full name?
A: Linda Hager Morse.
Q: Can you indicate something of your background and education?
A: I was born in Philadelphia, Pennsylvania. I went to high school there. While in high school I was a Merit Scholarship semi-finalist and was chairman of the Northwest Philadelphia Branch of the Junior Red Cross. As a result of that I won the Juvenile Decency Award from the Kiwanis Club, one of thirteen high school students in Philadelphia that year. . . .
I went to the University of New Hampshire after graduating from high school and stayed there for two years. I studied biology while I was there. Then I left college and went back to Philadelphia and worked for several years in a community organizing project for a non-violent pacifist group called Fellowship House in the black community of Philadelphia. Then I went to New York City and started working for the Fifth Avenue Vietnam Peace Parade Committee in 1965 which was the first coalition organization to organize the mass anti-war marches starting that year. . . .

1   Mr. William Kunstler was one of the defense attorneys.

Cross Examination

By Mr. Schultz [2]

Q: You practice shooting an M-1 [rifle] yourself, don't you?
A: Yes, I do.
Q: You also practice karate, don't you?
A: Yes, I do.
Q: What else do you practice?
A: Just those two things.
Q: That is for the revolution, isn't it?
A: After Chicago I changed from being a pacifist to the realization we had to defend ourselves. A non-violent revolution was impossible. I desperately wish it was possible.
Q: And the only way you can change this country, is it not, is by a violent revolution, isn't that your thought?
A: I desperately wish we could change it by a non-violent revolution, sir.
Q: Please, answer my question.
The Court: Read the question to the witness, please. (Record read)

A: I believe we have to have a revolution that changes the society into a good society, and to a society that meets the ideals that the country was founded on years ago which it hasn't met since then, and I think that we have the right to defend ourselves. The Minutemen in New York City were arrested with bazookas. Housewives in suburban areas have guns.
Q: And the way you are going to change this country is by violent revolution, isn't that right, Miss Morse?
A: The way we are going to change the country is by political revolution, sir.
Q: Miss Morse, isn't it a fact that in your opinion, there is no alternative but revolution?
A: Yes.
Q: Isn't it a fact, Miss Morse, that on a previous occasion you stated that the revolution will be gradual and that the people will gain control of sections of the city, just as the people of the National Liberation Front?
A: Yes, I believe so.

2   Mr. Richard G. Schultz, Assistant United States Attorney, was one of the attorneys for the prosecution.

Q: Isn't it a fact that you believe that the United States Government will control sections of its cities while the fighting rages in other sections of the cities not controlled by the Government of the United States?

A: That the Government of the United States has lost its credibility today; that there is fighting in the United States today going on in cities in this country today. People's Park in Berkeley, the policemen shot at us when people were unarmed, were fighting, if you wish, with rocks, the policemen used double-load buckshot and rifles, and pistols against unarmed demonstrators. That is fighting, OK? There is fighting going on in the United States right now. People are fighting to regain their liberty, fighting to regain their freedom, fighting for a totally different society, people in the black community, people in the Puerto Rican community, people in the Mexican-American community, and people in the white communities. They are fighting by political means as well as defending themselves.

Mr. Schultz: Your Honor, that is not an answer to my question. My question was whether or not she—

The Court: I know what your question was, and I agree it was not an answer. I direct the reporter to read it again, and— this may be funny to you. It isn't to me.

Mr. Kunstler: Your Honor, you can't characterize every facial expression as being funny.

The Court: But she is smiling. I never smile unless I think something is funny; but I am putting aside the question of whether or not it is funny. She is an intelligent young woman. She is able to hear and I want her to answer that question, if she can. If she feels she cannot answer, she may say I cannot answer that question.

Mr. Kunstler: Your Honor, they are intensely political questions and she is trying to give a political answer to a political question.

The Court: This is not a political case as far as I am concerned.

Mr. Kunstler: Well, your Honor, as far as some of the rest of us are concerned, it is quite a political case.

The Court: It is a criminal case. There is an indictment here. I have the indictment right up here. I can't go into politics here in this court.

Mr. Kunstler: Your Honor, Jesus was accused criminally, too, and we understand really that was not truly a criminal case in the sense that it is just an ordinary—

The Court: I didn't live at that time. I don't know. Some people think I go back that far, but I really didn't.

Mr. Kunstler: Well, I was assuming your Honor had read of the incident.

The Court: I would say that all we are dealing with here now is a cross examination of a witness, and I direct you to answer the question when it is read to you again. (Question read)

A: Yes, but the statement is taken out of context.

By Mr. Schultz

Q: Isn't it a fact that you have stated in a previous occasion that there will be sections that we will gain control over as the National Liberation Front has done in the villages of Viet Nam, and sections that Washington still dominates, as it does the area around Saigon, and sections where the fighting continues to rage?

A: Yes, I believe that there would be sections of the country that the people of the United States regain control of, and sections of the country that Washington, D.C., will control with its police and its troops, and sections where there will be a conflict.

Q: And gradually the Government of the United States will be taken over by this revolution?

A: Yes.

Q: And that your ultimate goal is to create a nation with this revolutionary party?

A: Revolutionary party? My ultimate goal is to create a society that is a free society; that is a joyous society where everyone is fed, where everyone is educated, where everyone has a job, where everyone has a chance to express himself artistically or politically, or spiritually, or religiously.

Q: With regard to the revolution that we are talking about, you are prepared, aren't you, both to die and to kill for it, isn't that right?

A: Yes.

The Court: I didn't hear that last answer.

A: I said yes, in self-defense.

Q: And further, because the educational system is so rotten, that if you cannot change it you will attempt to totally destroy it in the United States, isn't that right?

A: The educational system in the United States right now is destroying millions of people in Vietnam and around the world. The aerosol bombs that are used in Vietnam, or are being prepared to be used in Vietnam for CBW warfare were prepared right at Berkeley, California, where I live, and the educational system in the country is used currently to destroy people, not to create life. . . . I believe we have to stop the murder of people around the world and in the United States, and when the educational system of this country participates in it technologically, yes, we have to put our bodies in the way and stop that process.

Q: And if necessary, totally destroy the educational system in the United States?

A: The parts that are doing that, yes. The technological brain power of the United States, the parts that are creating CBW warfare, that are creating counter insurgency techniques for the black community, for South Africa, for Viet Nam, for Latin America, and for this country.

Q: One of the reasons further for your revolution is your opposition to capitalism and imperialism, isn't that right?

A: That's right.

Q: That is capitalism of the United States and the imperialism of the United States, isn't that right?

A: The systems in the United States which are—

Q: No, no. Please listen to my question. If it requires elaboration, please elaborate, but my question to you is, the capitalism and imperialism which you want to destroy is that capitalism and imperialism of the United States.

A: That is correct.

Q: And the more you realize our system is sick, the more you want to tear it limb to limb, isn't that right?

A: The more that I see the horrors that are perpetuated by this Government, the more that I read about things like troop trains full of nerve gas traveling across the country where one accident could wipe out thousands and thousands of people, the more that I see things like companies just pouring waste into lakes and into rivers and just destroying them, the more I see things like the oil fields in the ocean off Santa Barbara coast where the Secretary of the Interior and the oil companies got together and agreed to continue producing oil from those off-shore oil fields and ruined a whole section of the coast; the more I see things like an educational system which teaches black people and Puerto Rican people and Mexican-Americans that they are only fit to be domestics and dishwashers, if that; the more that I see a system that teaches middle class whites like me that we are supposed to be technological brains to continue producing CBW warfare, to continue working on computers and things like that to learn how to kill people better, to learn how to control people better, yes, the more I want to see that system torn down and replaced by a totally different one; one that cares about people learning; that cares about children being fed breakfast before they go to school; one that cares about people going to college for free; one that cares about people living adult lives that are responsible, fulfilled adult lives, not just drudgery, day after day after day going to a job; one that gives people a chance to express themselves artistically and politically, and religiously and philosophically. That is the kind of system I want to see in its stead.

Mr. Schultz: Your Honor, the answer is not responsive. I move it be stricken.

Mr. Kunstler: The answer could not have been more responsive to his question.

The Court: Not much more. I strike the answer and direct the jury to disregard it as being unresponsive to the question.

Mr. Schultz: May the court reporter read the question to the witness again?

The Court: Yes, indeed. Please read the question. Listen carefully, Miss Witness. You are a very articulate person. I am interested but I have got to control this trial according to the rules of evidence. Did you ever hear of the rules of evidence?

The Witness: No, I haven't.

A: The more I want to change it completely, yes.

Q: Isn't it a fact that on a prior occasion you have said that the more you realize society is sick, the more you want to tear it from limb to limb?

A: Yes.

Q: Now isn't it a fact, Miss Morse, that your feeling is that this country is going to have to be changed radically and the way this is going to come about is through a revolution and this revolution is going to entail the use of violence on both—on our part both to defend ourselves and to tear down the establishment?

A: Yes, that is correct.

Q: And, isn't it a fact, Miss Morse, that your learning your karate and your other skill is to use these skills in revolutionary guerrilla warfare on the streets of the American cities?

A: I still don't know whether I could ever kill anyone, Mr. Schultz.

Q: Well let me ask you—

A: I haven't reached that point yet.

Q: Your feeling is, Miss Morse, that you cannot make the people aware of the sickness in America without your revolution, isn't that right?

A: Before you can change people . . . or change society, you have to make people aware of the sickness in the society and . . . the only solution to those sicknesses is a revolution, but that is not the same as saying that you have to have a revolution first and then people will become aware. It is impossible to have a revolution unless all of the people want it. . . .

People make the revolution. A small band of radicals like the stereotype doesn't make a revolution. It is the masses of American people or all of the Vietnamese people. And the revolution won't happen until everyone or practically everyone in the country wants it except those opposed to it who have the most to lose.

Redirect Examination

By Mr. Kunstler

Q: Can you state to the jury what your views were on the same subject as Mr. Schultz related to you prior to the Democratic National Convention in 1968?

A: Prior to the Democratic convention I had believed that the United States' society system had to be changed, the economic and political system, but the way to bring about that change was through non-violent means, non-violent action, and through political organizing. I felt that we could reach policemen, that we could reach the Government of the United States by holding non-violent sit-ins and non-violent demonstrations, by putting our bodies on the line and allowing ourselves to be beaten if they chose to do that, and I have been beaten several times during such demonstrations, and not fighting back and showing that we could create a different kind of society that way, a society of love and change the policemen's attitudes toward us and the attitudes of the Government towards us, you know, by loving them.

Q: Can you state to the Judge and jury, Miss Morse, what caused a change in your thinking of this same subject?

A: The Democratic Convention Week. I have been to hundreds of demonstrations—

Mr. *Schultz:* Object. The witness has answered the question.

By Mr. *Kunstler*

Q: Can you explain to the jury why your attitude toward your country and the world changed because of the Democratic Convention Week?

A: The specific things that made me change my attitude were the actions of Mayor Daley's part; in refusing to give us permits, in violating completely as far as I was concerned, the Constitution which allows you the right to march and demonstrate, the actions on the part of the policemen and some of the National Guardsmen, although not all of them—some of them were great—in beating demonstrators horribly, and preventing us from exercising our Constitutional rights, and what I saw on television of what was going on inside the Convention which convinced me that the democratic process, political process, had fallen apart; that the police state that existed outside the Convention also existed inside the Convention and that non-violent methods would not work to change that; that we had to defend ourselves or we would be wiped out.

Q: By the way, how old are you?

A: Twenty-six years old. Just twenty-six.

"Thoughts on Dissent and Protest,"
Senator Edward M. Kennedy (D., Mass.)

The following are excerpts from remarks made by Senator Edward M. Kennedy before a Senate subcommittee investigating federal handling of demonstrations in June 1970. In his remarks he affirms the rights of dissenters to

Remarks by Senator Edward M. Kennedy as found in "Federal Handling of Demonstrations," Hearings before the Subcommittee on Administrative Practice and Procedure of the Committee on the Judiciary of the U.S. Senate, 91st Congress, 2nd Session, Part 1 (June 10, 1970), pp. 1–2.

protest even at the seat of the nation's government and forcefully condemns the use of violence. A comparison of Senator Kennedy's reflections on the use of violence with Ms. Morse's views reveal vastly different assumptions about the nature of American society and its ability to permit and respond to dissent.

Many of us in public life have found it necessary in recent months to focus on, and decry, the growing polarization in our society, and to criticize those who have contributed to it. For there are enough issues to disagree about in our nation, and enough people to disagree about them, without having those disagreements personalized and emotionalized and exaggerated.

And perhaps because we have spent so much effort either polarizing, or decrying polarization, we seem to have lost sight of the values and goals and traditions and hopes that we all have in common, the things we agree on, the facts of life which bring us together.

The American flag, for example, is a cherished symbol for all of us. Though some elements have attempted to adopt it as their own, and have sought to identify it with a particular philosophy or attitude or group, the fact is that the flag represents the common history and ideals which join us, from the American Revolution to the first men on the moon. It speaks not of current policies or present leaders, but of enduring principles and permanent norms. No American, no matter what his position on the Indo-China War, or on the other pressing issues of the 1970's, need be embarrassed to show his flag on Flag Day this Sunday, or on any other day, for the flag stands for all that is right and good and just in America. On the other hand, no American becomes more patriotic or more correct in his views or more worthy of public respect merely because he carries a flag; his ideas and deeds and statements must stand or fall on their own merits, whatever symbol he carries.

So, too, today we are focusing on two principles which unite us, and which make our flag and our nation stand tall; first, the right of all Americans to assemble to express their views freely and openly, no matter how unpopular those views may be; and, second, society's right to public safety and its rejection of violence as a means even to the most desirable ends.

For the most part, the antiwar demonstration in Washington on May 9 [1970] proved that these two basic themes of American life are neither inconsistent nor incompatible. We can have dissent, even massive dissent, and even right at the seat of our government without a threat to our security. We can let all types of philosophy compete in the marketplace of ideas, as our Constitution intended, without risking community stability. And at the same time we can protect ourselves against those few who take advantage of mass gatherings to cloak their own violent activities, and we can do so without allowing the peacekeepers to become violent themselves.

For violence between Americans—between demonstrators and policemen, or between demonstrators and counterdemonstrators, or by demonstrators upon private and public property —is unequivocably unacceptable as a mode of expression, a means of dissent, or a tool of vengeance. Violence is an admission that one's ideas and goals cannot prevail on their own merits. Violence short circuits the human power of verbalization. It carries in its wake not progress and movement and change, but tragedy and repression and social shock.

Thus we must learn well the lessons of how we can allow and encourage dissent without citizen violence, and how we can maintain order and safety without social violence.

Chapter 6

When Should Society

Restrict Dissent?

Dissent and protest can be expensive even if one excludes psychic damages and concentrates solely upon material costs. For example, costs of a two-day anti-war demonstration in Washington, D.C., in May 1970, a demonstration cited by Senator Edward M. Kennedy as a fine example of massive protest in which the interests both of the dissenters and of the society are protected, totaled $63,394 (see Table 6.1). A more costly protest in

Table 6.1. Costs of a Demonstration in Washington, D.C., May 9–10, 1970, to the National Park Service, National Capital Parks

Policing:	
Regular time salary costs	$ 8,569
Overtime salary costs	26,092
Other costs	3,466
Total	38,127
Providing platforms, sound equipment, comfort station facilities, and snow fence	12,597
Cleanup of grounds	2,225
Added cost of operating and protecting memorials	1,105
Estimated cost for repair and restoration of park facilities:	
Turf	1,050
Reflecting Pool	1,926
Other pools and fountains	564
Washington Monument	600
Various statues and monuments due to defacement	2,700
Trash baskets	2,500
Total	9,340
Total	63,394

Source: "Federal Handling of Demonstrations," p. 84.

that same city involved the seizure and occupation of the Bureau of Indian Affairs in November 1972, the six-day occupation resulting in damages in excess of $500,000. And after the 1967 civil disturbances, a study by a Senate subcommittee reported 83 deaths, 1,897 injuries, and substantial property damage (e.g., Detroit—$40–45 million; Newark—$10.2 million; and Cincinnati—more than $1 million).

Dissent and protest can also be upsetting, annoying, and irksome when it is disruptive of normal activities, or when it is directed against ideas, institutions, or individuals one supports and encourages, or when it involves one in a direct confrontation with the dissenter himself. For, as Senator Sam Ervin remarked at another Senate subcommittee hearing:

> The first amendment grants its freedoms to all persons within the boundaries of our country without regard to whether they are wise or foolish, learned or ignorant, profound or shallow, brave or timid, or devout or ungodly, and without regard to whether they love or hate our country and its institutions. Consequently, the amendment protects the expression of all kinds of ideas, no matter how antiquated, novel, or queer they may be.

Dissent and protest can also be a threat to the security of the individual and the state when it is used to justify the commission of violent or criminal acts. The willful destruction of property by bombings, arson, or vandalism, the assassination of individuals, and the hampering of those areas vital to the maintenance of the state pose serious dilemmas for a society, particularly a society such as that found in the United States which guarantees the freedom of dissent in the First Amendment to the Constitution.

The exercise of dissent and protest brings into conflict two basic rights within a society—the right of citizens to dissent and the right of a government to protect its citizens and its property. While in the United States freedom of thought is absolute, other First Amendment freedoms are not. As a result of constitutional interpretations by the Supreme Court of the United States, the government may in certain circumstances restrict the free exercise of First Amendment rights. Over a number of years, the Supreme Court has established guidelines for such restrictions. For example, one may not engage in the exercise of speech, association, or assembly which libels or slanders others, incites others to violence, obstructs the courts, constitutes sedition, or otherwise endangers the national security.

Although at first glance these guidelines may appear to be rather clear and definitive in establishing a proper balance, upon closer examination the guidelines are actually quite nebulous. What endangers national security? Does an anti-war demonstration in Washington, D.C.? Does a meeting of the Black Panthers, the SDS, or the Communist party? What constitutes inciting to violence? Does a speech urging a group to conduct a protest march? Does a demonstration for racial integration which antagonizes onlookers? When *does* dissent become dangerous so that it must be restricted?

The remainder of this chapter consists of a series of actual cases and resulting Supreme Court decisions. All of them deal with the efforts of a dissenting citizen or group of dissenting citizens to protest some action, and thus they present real dilemmas with respect to the rights and responsibilities of citizens and the society.

For each case, assume the role of a judge. Using the facts provided in the scenario and ensuing decisions, indicate the decision you would render and, more importantly, the reasons for your decision. Notice that following all of the case scenarios, excerpts of two decisions are provided, one in support of the convicted individual or petitioner, and the other in support of the government or respondent. In each case, one decision is taken from the actual majority or concurring opinion rendered by the Supreme Court in the case. The other is either a dissenting opinion or a facsimile of a dissent. (Identification of the actual decisions is made at the end of the chapter.)

When Should Free Speech Be Restricted?
(Feiner v. New York, 1950)

When Syracuse city officials cancelled a permit for a former assistant attorney general to speak in a public-school building on the subject of racial discrimination and civil liberties, the Young Progressives, the sponsoring organization, arranged for the speech to be given at a city hotel. Disturbed by the cancellation, Irving Feiner, a young Syracuse University student, decided to protest the actions of city officials and publicize the new meeting-place. He stood on a large wooden box on a city sidewalk and spoke to passers-by through a loudspeaker.

In his speech, Feiner made derogatory remarks about President Truman, the American Legion, the Mayor of Syracuse, and other local political officials. He also spoke out against racial discrimination and urged black people to stand up and fight for equal rights. Feiner soon attracted a crowd—some black, some white—which became increasingly restless as Feiner continued to speak.

After almost one-half hour of Feiner's speech, the police, who had been observing the proceedings, asked Feiner to stop speaking, fearful that the crowd would become violent. After refusing three times to stop speaking, Feiner was arrested by the police and charged with disorderly conduct. Convicted on the grounds that his speech presented a clear danger of disorder on the streets, Feiner appealed to a federal court charging that his First Amendment rights had been violated. May police stop a speaker if they disagree with what he is saying? If, in the course of a speech, the audience begins to react emotionally, to whom do the police have the more basic obligation? Should they protect the speaker from the crowd or the crowd from the speaker? You are the judge; how would you rule?

Decision for the Petitioner (Feiner)

Public assemblies and public speech occupy an important role in American life. One high function of the police is to protect these lawful gatherings so that the speakers may exercise their constitutional rights. When unpopular causes are sponsored from the public platform there will commonly be mutterings and unrest and heckling from the crowd. When a speaker mounts a platform it is not unusual to find him resorting to exaggeration, to vilification of ideas and men, to the making of false charges. But those extravagances . . . do not justify penalizing the speaker by depriving him of the platform or by punishing him for his conduct.

A speaker may not, of course, incite a riot. . . . But this record shows no such extremes. It shows an unsympathetic audience and the threat of one man to haul the speaker from the stage. It is against that kind of threat that speakers need police protection. If they do not receive it and instead the police throw their weight on the side of those who would break up the meetings, the police become the new censors of speech. Police censorship has all the vices of censorship from city halls which we have repeatedly struck down. . . . Reversed.

Decision for the Respondent (New York)

The courts below recognized petitioner's right to hold a street meeting at this locality, to make use of loud-speaking equipment in giving his speech, and to make derogatory remarks concerning public officials and the American Legion. They found that the officers in making the arrest were motivated solely by a proper concern for the preservation of order and protection of the general welfare, and that there was no evidence which could lend color to a claim that the acts of the police were a cover for suppression of petitioner's views and opinions. Petitioner was thus neither arrested nor convicted for the making or the content of his speech. Rather, it was the reaction which it actually engendered.

. . . The findings of the New York courts as to the condition of the crowd and the refusal of petitioner to obey the police requests, supported as they are by the record of this case, are persuasive that the conviction of petitioner for violation of public peace, order and authority does not exceed the bounds of proper state police action. This Court respects, as it must, the interest of the community in maintaining peace and order on its streets. . . . It is one thing to say that the police cannot be used as an instrument for the suppression of unpopular views, and another to say that, when as here the speaker passes the bounds of argument or persuasion and undertakes incitement to riot, they are powerless to prevent a breach of the peace. . . . Affirmed.

When Should Free Speech and Assembly Be Restricted? (Edwards v. South Carolina, 1963)

After gathering in the morning at the Zion Baptist Church in Columbia, a number of black. high-school and college students walked in separate groups of about fifteen to the South Carolina State House grounds a few blocks away from the church. Their purpose was to protest discrimination in general against the black citizens of South Carolina and, more specifically, to demonstrate their desire to eliminate those laws which prohibited blacks from securing equal privileges in the state.

After arriving at the State House grounds, the demonstrators were met by thirty or more policemen who requested them to walk peacefully and not obstruct either pedestrians or vehicles. They began to walk in single file or two abreast in an orderly way carrying with them placards reading "Down with segregation" and other slogans.

These actions attracted a crowd of between two and three hundred onlookers. Although at the time there was no evidence of hostility by the onlookers—no threatening remarks, hostile gestures, or offensive language—the police feared that the situation could ultimately erupt in disorder and violence. Consequently, the police asked the demonstrators to disperse within fifteen minutes or face arrest. Instead of complying with the wishes of the police, the demonstrators responded with loud singing of various patriotic and religious songs accompanied by the clapping of their hands and stomping of their feet.

After fifteen minutes, the police moved in and arrested the demonstrators, charging them with breach of the peace. Convicted, they appealed the decision, contending that their arrest by the police represented an infringement of their constitutionally protected rights of free speech, free assembly, and freedom to petition for the redress of grievances. You are the judge; how would you rule?

Decision for the Petitioner (Edwards)

It has long been established that these First Amendment freedoms are protected by the Fourteenth Amendment from invasion by the States. The circumstances in this case reflect an exercise of these basic constitutional rights in their most pristine and classic form. The petitioners felt aggrieved by laws of South Carolina which allegedly "prohibited Negro privileges in this State." They peaceably assembled at the site of the State Government and there peaceably expressed their grievances "to the citizens of South Carolina, along with the Legislative Bodies of South Carolina." Not until they were told by police officials that they must disperse on pain of arrest did they do more. Even then, they but sang patriotic and religious songs after one of their leaders had delivered a "religious harangue." There was no violence or threat of violence on their part, or on the part of any member of the crowd watching them. Police protection was "ample."

. . . These petitioners were convicted of an offense so generalized as to be, in the words of the South Carolina Supreme Court, "not susceptible of exact definition." And they were con-

victed upon evidence which showed no more than that the opinions which they were peaceably expressing were sufficiently
opposed to the views of the majority of the community to attract
a crowd and necessitate police protection.

The Fourteenth Amendment does not permit a State to
make criminal the peaceful expression of unpopular views. . . .
A statute which upon its face, and as authoritatively construed,
is so vague and indefinite as to permit the punishment of the
fair use of this opportunity is repugnant to the guaranty of liberty
contained in the Fourteenth Amendment. . . . Reversed.

Decision for the Respondent (South Carolina)

The question . . . seems . . . whether a State is constitutionally prohibited from enforcing laws to prevent breach of the
peace in a situation where city officials in good faith believe, and
the record shows, that disorder and violence are imminent,
merely because the activities constituting that breach contain
claimed elements of constitutionally protected speech and assembly. To me the answer under our cases is clearly in the
negative. . . .

Here 200 youthful Negro demonstrators were being aroused
to a "fever pitch" before a crowd of some 300 people who undoubtedly were hostile. Perhaps their speech was not so animated
but in this setting their actions, their placards . . . and their
chanting . . . accompanied by stamping feet and clapping hands,
created . . . danger of riot and disorder. . . . Anyone conversant
with the almost spontaneous combustion in some Southern communities in such a situation will agree that the City Manager's
action may well have averted a major catastrophe.

. . . to say that the police may not intervene until the riot has
occurred is like keeping out the doctor until the patient dies. . . .

It is not a constitutional principle that, in acting to preserve
order, the police must proceed against the crowd, whatever its
size and temper, and not against the [demonstrators]. . . . af-
firm the convictions.

May a State Limit Places of Protest?
(Adderley v. Florida, 1966)

Following the arrest of some of their schoolmates the previous day for their attempts to integrate public theaters, a large

number of Florida A. &. M. students gathered on the campus to discuss the situation. Approximately two hundred students decided to march to the county jail and there to protest those arrests and to demonstrate in general against state and local policies and practices of racial segregation, including segregation of the jail itself.

As they arrived on the jail premises they began to demonstrate peaceably. In the absence of the sheriff, a deputy sheriff met with the group and asked them to move back away from the jail. They complied with this request by moving back somewhat but they still remained on jail premises, where they stood or sat while singing and clapping.

When the sheriff arrived, the demonstration was in full progress. The sheriff met with leaders of the demonstration and advised them that they were not only blocking a driveway leading up to the entrance of the jail, but that they were illegally on jail premises. He ordered the demonstrators to disperse or face arrest for trespassing on county property in violation of the law.

While some of the demonstrators left, the majority remained, insisting that they had a constitutional right to remain on the jail premises because the jail grounds were both reasonable and particularly appropriate for their demonstration. The sheriff proceeded to arrest a total of 107 demonstrators. Convicted, they appealed to a federal court. You are the judge; how would you rule?

Decision for the Petitioner (Adderley)

The jailhouse, like an executive mansion, a legislative chamber, a courthouse, or the statehouse itself is one of the seats of government, whether it be the Tower of London, the Bastille, or a small county jail. And when it houses political prisoners or those who many think are unjustly held, it is an obvious center for protest. . . .

There is no question that petitioners had as their purpose a protest against the arrest of Florida A. & M. students for trying to integrate public theaters. . . . There was no violence; no threat of violence; no attempted jail break; no storming of a prison; no plan or plot to do anything but protest. The evidence is uncontradicted that the petitioners' conduct did not upset the jailhouse routine; things went on as they normally would. . . . If there was congestion, the solution was a further request to move to lawns or parking areas, not complete ejection and arrest.

. . . Saying that the "custodian" of the public property in his discretion can decide when public places shall be used for the communication of ideas, especially the constitutional right to assemble and petition for redress of grievances . . . is to place those who assert their First Amendment rights at his mercy. It gives him the awesome power to decide whose ideas may be expressed and who shall be denied a place to air their claims and petition their government. . . .

Today a trespass law is used to penalize a people for exercising a constitutional right. Tomorrow a disorderly conduct statute, a breach-of-the-peace statute, a vagrancy statute will be put to the same end. . . . By allowing these orderly and civilized protests against injustice to be suppressed, we only increase the forces of frustration which the conditions of second-class citizenship are generating amongst us. Reverse the convictions.

Decision for the Respondents (Florida)

. . . South Carolina sought to prosecute its State Capitol demonstrators by charging them with the common-law crime of breach of the peace. This Court in Edwards took pains to point out at length the indefinite, loose, and broad nature of this charge; indeed . . . South Carolina's power to prosecute, it was emphasized, would have been different had the State proceeded under a "precise and narrowly drawn regulatory statute evincing a legislative judgment that certain specific conduct be limited or proscribed" such as, for example, "limiting the periods during which the State House grounds were open to the public. . . ."

The Florida trespass statute under which these petitioners were charged cannot be challenged on this ground. It is aimed at conduct of one limited kind, that is, for one person or persons to trespass upon the property of another with a malicious and mischievous intent. There is no lack of notice in this law, nothing to entrap or fool the unwary.

. . . Nothing in the Constitution of the United States prevents Florida from even-handed enforcement of its general trespass statute against those refusing to obey the sheriff's order to remove themselves from what amounted to the curtilage of the jailhouse. The State, no less than a private owner of property, has power to preserve the property under its control for the use to which it is lawfully dedicated. For this reason there is no merit to the petitioners' argument that they had a constitutional right to stay on the property, over the jail custodian's objections, because this "area chosen for the peaceful civil rights demonstration was not only 'reasonable' but also particularly appropriate. . . ." Such an argument has as its major unarticulated premise the assumption that people who want to propagandize protests or views have a constitutional right to do so whenever and however and wherever they please. . . . We reject [that concept]. . . . The United States Constitution does not forbid a State to control the use of its own property for its own lawful nondiscriminatory purpose. Affirmed.

When Protest Arouses Reaction, Who Is To Be Protected? (Gregory v. Chicago, 1969)

Dissatisfied with the city of Chicago's efforts to desegregate its public schools, a number of people gathered in Chicago's Grant Park to hear nationally known civil-rights activist Dick Gregory. Mr. Gregory urged the group to march peaceably first to city hall and then to Mayor Richard Daley's home, some five miles away, to demonstrate their concern with the situation in the public schools and to demand to have the Mayor remove the present Superintendent of Schools. Accompanied by the police and the Assistant City Attorney, the demonstrators, numbering about 85, proceeded in an orderly and peaceful march to the Mayor's home, arriving there about 8:00 P.M. As they began marching around near the Mayor's home, they attracted a crowd of neighborhood spectators who were generally unsympathetic with the demonstrators, a crowd that grew increasingly more hostile, both in language and in conduct, as the demonstration continued. Finally, at about 9:30 P.M., fearful that the threatening crowd of onlookers could no longer be contained, the police asked Dick Gregory and the other marchers to leave the area. When they refused, they were arrested and charged with violation of Chicago's disorderly-conduct ordinance. Convicted, the defendants appealed to the federal courts. In a situation like this, to whom does society have the more basic responsibility—the demonstrators or "the citizens of Chicago"? You are the judge; how would you rule?

Decision for the Petitioner (Gregory)

. . . While we have pointed out in many cases that the States, and their subordinate units, do have constitutional power to regulate picketing, demonstrating, and parading by statutes and ordinances narrowly drawn so as not to abridge the rights of speech, press, assembly, or petition, neither Chicago nor Illinois at the time these petitioners were demonstrating had passed any such narrowly drawn laws.

. . . Outside of the marching and propagandizing of their views and protests, Gregory and his group while marching did all in their power to maintain order. Indeed, in the face of jeers, insults, and assaults with rocks and eggs, Gregory and his group maintained a decorum that speaks well for their determination simply to tell their side of their grievances and complaints. . . . Thus both police and demonstrators made their best efforts faithfully to discharge their responsibilities as officers and citizens, but they were nevertheless unable to restrain the hostile hecklers within decent and orderly bounds. These facts disclosed by the record point unerringly to one conclusion, namely, that when groups with diametrically opposed, deep-seated views are permitted to air their emotional grievances, side by side, on city streets, tranquility and order cannot be maintained even by the joint efforts of the finest and best officers and of those who desire to be the most law-abiding protestors of their grievances.

It is because of this truth, and a desire both to promote order and to safeguard First Amendment freedoms, that this Court has repeatedly warned States and governmental units that they cannot regulate a conduct connected with these freedoms through use of sweeping, dragnet statutes that may, because of vagueness, jeopardize these freedoms. . . . Reversed.

Decision for the Respondent (Chicago)

Freedom of speech, press, assembly, or petition can [not] be abridged so long as the First Amendment remains unchanged in our Constitution. But to say that the First Amendment grants those broad rights free from an exercise of governmental power to regulate conduct, as distinguished from speech, press, assembly or petition, would subject all the people of the nation to the uncontrollable whim and arrogance of speakers, and writers, and protesters, and grievance bearers. . . .

Were the authority of government so trifling as to permit anyone with a complaint to have the vast power to do anything he pleased, wherever he pleased, and whenever he pleased, our customs and habits of conduct, social, political, economic, ethical, and religious, would all be wiped out, and become no more than relics of a gone but not forgotten past. Churches would be compelled to welcome into their buildings invaders who came but to scoff and jeer; streets and highways and public buildings would cease to be available for the purposes for which they were constructed and dedicated whenever demonstrators and picketers wanted to use them for their own purposes. And perhaps worse than all other changes, homes, the sacred retreat to which families repair for their privacy and their daily way of living, would have to have their doors thrown open to all who desired to convert the occupants to new views, new morals, and a new way of life. Men and women who hold public office would be compelled, simply because they did hold public office, to lose the comforts and privacy of an unpicketed home. . . . Our Constitution . . . did not create a government with such monumental weaknesses. Speech and press are, of course, to be free, so that public matters can be discussed with impunity. But picketing and demonstrating can be regulated like other conduct of men. I believe that the homes of men, sometimes the last citadel of the tired, the weary, and the sick, can be protected by government from noisy, marching, tramping, threatening picketers and demonstrators bent on filling the minds of men, women, and children with fears of the unknown. . . .

May a License Be Required for the Exercise of Free Speech? Is One Ever Justified in Breaking a Law? (Shuttlesworth v. Birmingham, 1969)

When some of the black residents, headed by the Reverend Fred Shuttlesworth, wished to protest the denial of civil rights to black citizens in the city of Birmingham by engaging in peaceful picketing, they sent a representative to apply for a parade permit. The representative met with the City Commissioner of Public Safety, Mr. Eugene "Bull" Conner, but was unable to secure the necessary permit. Two days later, The Rev. Mr. Shuttlesworth sent a telegram to Commissioner Conner requesting a permit to picket "against the injustices of segregation and discrimination," specifying where the picketing would occur and agreeing to abide by normal rules governing picketing groups. Replying by telegram, Commissioner Conner indicated that he did not have the authority to grant the parade permit, for it was necessary for the entire Commission to do so, and concluded with the statement: "I insist that you and your people do not start any picketing on the streets in Birmingham, Alabama."

Faced with Commissioner Conner's refusal and admonition, and realizing that only one session of the City Commission was scheduled to meet before Good Friday, the day planned for the demonstration, the Rev. Mr. Shuttlesworth and his group decided to picket without the permit. Thus, on Good Friday, April 12, 1963, a group of about fifty black residents, including three ministers, left a Birmingham church, and began to walk in orderly fashion on the sidewalks, carefully obeying traffic signals and avoiding the obstruction of vehicular traffic. A crowd of spectators gathered some distance behind the marchers, although neither the marchers nor the crowd blocked the street or obstructed automobile traffic.

After walking for four blocks the police stopped the marchers and arrested them for violation of the city ordinance requiring a parade permit. Convicted, the Rev. Mr. Shuttlesworth appealed, arguing that the city commission had unconstitutionally denied him and his group their First Amendment rights by subjecting the exercise of those rights to prior restraint of a license or permit. He further contended that since the city ordinance was an invalid law, he was not compelled to obey it and thus could not be punished under it. The city officials of Birmingham argued that they had a right to restrict the use of the streets by the general public in connection with the safety, comfort, and convenience of the general public. You are the judge; how would you rule?

Decision for the Petitioner (Shuttlesworth)

There can be no doubt that the Birmingham ordinance, as it was written, conferred upon the City Commission virtually unbridled and absolute power to prohibit any "parade," "procession," or "demonstration" on the city's streets or public ways. For in deciding whether or not to withhold a permit, the members of the Commission were to be guided only by their own ideas of "public welfare, peace, safety, health, decency, good order,

morals or convenience." This ordinance as it was written, therefore, fell squarely within the ambit of the many decisions of this
Court over the last 30 years, holding that a law subjecting the
exercise of First Amendment freedoms to the prior restraint of a
license, without narrow, objective, and definite standards to
guide the licensing authority, is unconstitutional. . . . And our
decisions have made clear that a person faced with such an unconstitutional licensing law may ignore it and engage with
impunity in the exercise of the right of free expression for which
the law purports to require a license. . . .

It is argued, however, that what was involved here was
not "pure speech," but the use of public streets and sidewalks,
over which a municipality must rightfully exercise a great
deal of control in the interest of traffic regulation and public
safety. That, of course, is true. . . .

But our decisions have also made clear that picketing
and parading may nonetheless constitute methods of expression,
entitled to First Amendment protection. . . . Even when the use
of its public streets and sidewalks is involved, therefore, a
municipality may not empower its licensing officials to roam
essentially at will, dispensing or withholding permission to speak,
assemble, picket, or parade, according to their own opinions regarding the potential effect of the activity in question on the
"welfare," "decency," or "morals" of the community. . . .
Reversed.

Decision for the Respondent (Birmingham)

While the petitioner suggests that the city ordinance in
question was a violation of the First Amendment guarantee of
free expression, we cannot concur. Clearly, as the Court has
indicated many times before, there is a difference between "pure
speech" and "picketing." The city ordinance was passed with a
valid concern for the "safety," "health," "good order," and "public welfare" of the community. Certainly that is a legitimate
concern. . . .

It should be pointed out that Rev. Shuttlesworth did not
comply with the requirements to secure a permit. He never made
application before the entire City Commission. To contend that
one is free to violate a city ordinance simply because of an
impression received in communication with a lesser city official

is to open the door to anarchy in this country. It would give the right of every individual to interpret laws by himself, a principle which cannot be tolerated in a lawful society. . . .

The decision in this case is far-reaching. It will be eagerly awaited by legally constituted authorities and those who seek to foster chaos and anarchy in this country. We can do nothing less . . . than to assert the fundamental principle of law involved. Authorities do have a proper concern with the use of public streets and thoroughfares. Individual citizens do have a responsibility to adhere to legally constituted statutes. Affirmed.

May Dissent and Protest Occur in Public Schools?
(Tinker v. Des Moines, 1969)

A group of adults and young people met in December 1965 for the purpose of publicizing their objections to the Vietnam war and their support for a truce. They decided that, beginning with a fast on December 16, they would wear black armbands during the holiday season, concluding their protest with a fast on December 31.

As word of their decision circulated, school principals in the Des Moines public schools learned of the plan. Fearing possible disturbances in the schools as a result of students wearing black armbands in the classroom, they adopted a policy on December 14 prohibiting the wearing of armbands in school, with failure to comply resulting in suspension.

Although aware of this new policy, both 13-year-old Mary Beth Tinker and 16-year-old Christopher Eckhardt wore black armbands to their schools on December 16. The next day, 15-year-old John Tinker also wore his armband to school. Altogether seven out of the school system's 18,000 pupils wore black armbands, including second-grade student Paul Tinker, eight years old, and fifth-grade student Hope Tinker, eleven years old. All seven students were suspended from school until they returned without their armbands. Refusing to comply, the students remained out of school for the period of time planned, not returning until after New Year's Day.

Through their fathers, the students sought a court injunction forbidding school officials from disciplining them, contending that the schools had denied them rights guaranteed in the First Amendment. School authorities disagreed, contending that their policy forbidding the wearing of black armbands was reasonable in order to prevent disturbance of school discipline. Does the wearing of a black armband come within the area of First Amendment protection? Do students have First Amendment freedoms in public schools? May school officials limit such freedoms to enforce school discipline and enforce reasonable policies to ensure the functioning of the schools? You are the judge; how would you rule?

Decision for the Petitioner (Tinker)

First Amendment rights, applied in light of the special characteristics of the school environment, are available to teachers and students. It can hardly be argued that either students or teachers shed their constitutional rights to freedom of speech or expression at the schoolhouse gate. This has been the unmistakable holding of this Court for almost 50 years. . . .

The District Court concluded that the action of the school authorities was reasonable because it was based upon their fear of a disturbance from the wearing of armbands. But, in our system, undifferentiated fear or apprehension of disturbance is not enough to overcome the right to freedom of expression. Any departure from absolute regimentation may cause trouble. Any variation from the majority's opinion may inspire fear. Any word spoken, in class, in the lunchroom, or on the campus, that deviates from the views of another person may start an argument or cause a disturbance. But our Constitution says we must take this risk. . . .

In order for the State in the person of school officials to justify prohibition of a particular expression or opinion, it must be able to show that its action was caused by something more than a mere desire to avoid the discomfort and unpleasantness that always accompany an unpopular viewpoint . . . that engaging in of the forbidden conduct would "materially and substantially interfere with the requirements of appropriate discipline in the operation of the school". . . .

In our system, state-operated schools may not be enclaves of totalitarianism. School officials do not possess absolute authority over their students. Students in school as well as out of school are "persons" under our Constitution. They are possessed of fundamental rights which the State must respect, just as they themselves must respect their obligations to the State. In our system, students may not be regarded as closed-circuit recipients of only that which the State chooses to communicate. They may not be confined to the expression of those sentiments that are officially approved. In the absence of a specific showing of constitutionally valid reasons to regulate their speech, students are entitled to freedom of expression of their views. . . . Reversed.

Decision for the Respondent (Des Moines)

. . . The record overwhelmingly shows that the armbands did exactly what the elected school officials and principals foresaw they would, that is, took the students' minds off their classwork and diverted them to thoughts about the highly emotional subject of the Vietnam war. . . . If the time has come when pupils of state-supported schools, kindergartens, grammar schools, or high schools, can defy and flout orders of school officials to keep their minds on their own schoolwork, it is the beginning of a new revolutionary era of permissiveness in this country fostered by the judiciary.

. . . It is a myth to say that any person has a constitutional right to say what he pleases, where he pleases, and when he pleases. Our Court has decided precisely the opposite.

. . . Teachers in state-controlled public schools are hired to teach there. . . . Certainly a teacher is not paid to go into school and teach subjects the State does not hire him to teach as a part of its selected curriculum. Nor are public school students sent to the schools at public expense to broadcast political or any other views to educate and inform the public. The original idea of schools . . . [not] yet abandoned as worthless or out of date, was that children had not yet reached the point of experience and wisdom which enabled them to teach all of their elders. It may be that the Nation has outworn the old-fashioned slogan that "children are to be seen, not heard," but one may, I hope, be permitted to harbor the thought that taxpayers send children to school on the premise that at their age they need to learn, not teach.

. . . School discipline, like parental discipline, is an integral and important part of training our children to be good citizens —to be better citizens. Here a very small number of students have crisply and summarily refused to obey a school order designed to give pupils who want to learn the opportunity to do so. . . . Students engaged in such activities are apparently confident that they know far more about how to operate public school systems than do their parents, teachers, and elected school officials. . . . Turned loose with lawsuits for damages and injunctions against their teachers as they are here, it is nothing but wishful thinking to imagine that young, immature students will not soon believe it is their right to control the schools rather than the right of the States that collect the taxes to hire the teachers for the benefit of the pupils. This case . . . subjects all the public schools in the country to the whims and caprices of their loudest-mouthed, but maybe not their brightest, students. . . . Decision upheld.

Supreme Court Decisions

The Supreme Court decided against Feiner (6–3), for Edwards (8–1), against Adderley (5–4), for Gregory (9–0), for Shuttlesworth (8–0), and for Tinker (7–2).

Chapter 7

How Should Society

Restrict Dissent?

Intimately connected with the question of when society should restrict dissent is the question of *how* society should restrict dissent. In the United States the question of when has been resolved largely by the judicial branch of government, whereas the question of how has been determined largely by the legislative and executive branches of government, particularly at the national level. It is, therefore, the actions of these branches which are essentially responsible for establishing the societal climate toward dissent and protest, whether that climate is one of receptivity or hostility.

Public Law 90–284

In the wake of the 1965 riot in Watts and the 1967 riots in almost 150 cities, a number of people in the United States clamored for ways to prevent similar outbreaks from recurring. Thus, in the spring of 1968, the United States Congress passed Public Law 90–284, the so-called anti-riot law. This law sought to restrict the freedom of prominent dissenters to travel freely within the country by providing that an individual may be subject to a $10,000 fine and/or five years in prison if he either travels between states or uses:

the mail, telegraph, telephone, radio, or television, with intent—(A) to incite a riot; or (B) to organize, promote, encourage, participate in, or carry on a riot; or (C) to commit any act of violence in furtherance of a riot; or (D) to aid or abet any person in inciting or participating in or

111

carrying on a riot or committing any act of violence in furtherance of a riot. . . .

Sponsor of this law in the House of Representatives, Rep. William Cramer (R.) of Florida, hypothesized that the riots had followed a similar pattern in most cities for they were planned by outside agitators and instigated by free-lance insurrectionists. He thus urged passage of the bill which he described as: "a bill of absolute necessity . . . that would protect the legitimate civil rights leaders in America and put the illegitimate, rabble-rousing, hatemongering so-called leaders out of business."

During the floor debate that ensued on the bill, a bill which Rep. Emanuel Cellar (D.) of New York characterized as "a futile gesture, neither preventative nor curative," Congressman Cellar pointed to what he considered to be several deficiencies in the proposed law. His main objection was the approach taken by the law, for he contended that what was needed was to take constructive action to eliminate the causes of black disaffection, to take positive action in such areas as poverty, housing, employment, and education, rather than simply to prescribe punishments for the results.

Maintaining that the proposed law would be virtually unenforcible, Rep. Cellar pointed to the difficulty of defining such words as "incite," "promote," and "encourage." How does this differ from "the mere advocacy of ideas or the mere expression of belief," both of which are constitutionally permissible? What criteria does one use to judge this?

Public Law 90–284 contains the following provision:

> Nothing contained in this section shall be construed to make it unlawful for any person to travel in, or use any facility of, interstate or foreign commerce for the purpose of pursuing the legitimate objectives of organized labor, through orderly and lawful means.

The sweeping nature of this law was such that labor leaders involved in normal union affairs could have been prosecuted, thus necessitating their specific exemption. But, while labor leaders have been exempted, other groups, such as civil-rights organizations, are vulnerable. In fact, this law, first applied in the famous Chicago 7 trial, makes it possible for a Vice President to be prosecuted for inciting a riot if he were to speak at a university in defense of American policy and a riot resulted. Does this law represent a valid approach to the problem of riots? Is this the way for society to limit dissent and protest?

Related to the intent of Public Law 90–284—to stop insurrectionists from moving freely throughout the country—is another approach by Congress, the publication of a list of "radical" speakers to discourage their appearance on college and university campuses. Prepared by the House Internal Security Committee, the report listed 65 individuals affiliated with one or more of the following groups (as quoted by David E. Rosenbaum in the New York *Times,* October 15, 1970):

1. Nation of Islam.
2. Communist party, USA.
3. National Committee to Abolish HUAC (House Un-American Activities Committee).
4. National Mobilization Committee To End the War in Vietnam.
5. Socialist Workers party.
6. Those cited for contempt in connection with the Chicago 7 conspiracy trial.
7. Black Panther party (supporter or member).
8. Students for a Democratic Society.
9. Student Nonviolent Coordinating Committee.
10. New Mobilization Committee To End the War in Vietnam.
11. Spring Mobilization Committee To End the War in Vietnam.
12. Youth International party (Yippies).

While the list included the names of Stokely Carmichael, Angela Davis, Abbie Hoffman, Mark Rudd, Jerry Rubin, William Kunstler, and others generally acknowledged to take or support "radical" positions, it also gave the names of some individuals who are not so acknowledged, including heavyweight boxer Muhammad Ali, poetry editor of the *Saturday Review,* John Ciardi, former Union Theological Seminary president, The Reverend John Bennett, and Task Force director, Jerome Skolnick. Despite efforts by the American Civil Liberties Union to prohibit the committee from publishing this list and a federal court order to prevent its release, the list was made public by committee chairman Rep. Richard Ichord (D.) of Missouri who claimed immunity from prosecution as a member of Congress. Is such an effort a valid measure to restrict dissent or does it violate the right of free speech and unduly harass those speakers with whom the government is in disagreement?

Examples of other attempts by members of Congress to restrict dissenters include the proceedings of the House Un-American Activities Committee, particularly during the 1950s, in its attempt to investigate Communism in the United States. A more recent example is the attempt, along with many state legislatures, to place strict limitations on protest activities and other related campus gatherings at the nation's colleges and universities by making such participants ineligible for national or state scholarship or loan assistance. Do laws of this nature provide proper protections for society or do they deny First Amendment protections?

Executive Order 11605

Since 1798, Congress has enacted legislation designed to protect this country from domestic danger. The 1798 Alien and Sedition Laws, the 1917–1918 Espionage and Sedition Laws, and the 1940 Smith Act have been among the most controversial of these laws. Following the heightened period of anti-Communism during the first half of the 1950s—the McCarthy era—a series of Supreme Court decisions effectively reduced the ability of Congress to restrict members of the Communist party, forbidding restrictions on the issuance of passports and the right to work in defense plants, and rescinding the requirement that members of the Communist party register with the United States government.

In the wake of mass dissent in the 1960s, President Richard Nixon on July 2, 1971, issued Executive Order 11605 in an attempt to revive the Subversive Activities Control Board, which had been originally set up by the Internal Security Act of 1950 to identify and require the public registration of Communists and Communist organizations. Supreme Court decisions had left that group virtually powerless, but the President sought to expand its authority by this executive order, which provided:

The Subversive Activities Control Board shall, upon petition of the Attorney General, conduct appropriate hearings to determine whether any organization is totalitarian, fascist, communist, subversive, or whether it has adopted a policy of unlawfully advocating the commission of acts of force or violence to deny others their rights under the Constitution or laws of the United States or of any State, or which seeks to overthrow the government of the United States or any State or subdivision thereof by unlawful means.

Senator Sam Ervin (D.) of North Carolina has expressed serious reservations about Executive Order 11605, charging that it represents a deliberate attempt by the executive branch to suppress dissent. Contending that such a group has no rightful place in America, Senator Ervin has stated:

> It is manifest, however, that the real objective of the order is to empower the Board to brand the organizations and groups specified in it as intellectually or politically dangerous to the established order. It is equally as manifest that such branding of these organizations and groups will place a political or social stigma on their members, and tend to minimize their exercise of freedom of speech, association, and assembly. . . .
>
> If America is to be free, her Government must permit her people to think their own thoughts and determine their own associations without official instruction or intimidation; and if America is to be secure, her Government must punish her people for the crimes they commit, not for the thoughts they think or the associations they choose.

Others, however, such as Senator Edward Gurney (R.) of Florida, have praised the President's effort as a legitimate exercise of government power to investigate and identify those groups which seek to overthrow the government and the institutions of American society. Senator Gurney has argued:

> This Nation has the right to defend itself, to prevent its destruction. Whether the attack is external or from within, the Government can and should insure the survival and stability of its institution. Moreover, the people of this Nation are entitled to have the background and character of Government employees thoroughly investigated. I do not believe that the taxpayers of this country should have to subsidize revolutionaries under the guise of protecting the first amendment right of freedom of speech and assembly by employing them as "civil servants." . . .
>
> I do not quarrel with the need to preserve the democratic framework of our society. I do not mean to in any way

minimize the importance of preserving full substantive and procedural due process of law. What I do mean to say is that the freedoms enumerated in the Bill of Rights are in no way synonymous with subversion. Nor were they designed by our Founding Fathers to provide full and absolute immunity to those engaged in subversion.

What do you think? Should a Subversive Activities Control Board exist and should it have the authority to investigate and identify groups it considers dangerous to the nation's security? Does such a group serve to protect the society from dangerous and subversive elements or does it really cloak unconstitutional methods to hamper the freedom of dissent?

May Day and Preventive Detention

In the spring of 1971, Washington, D.C., had been the center of anti-war demonstrations for several weeks, involving crowds of demonstrators in excess of 200,000. Some of the protest groups had threatened to close down the city and the government by clogging both the bridges and the main routes of the city to prevent people from reporting to work. In face of the onset of the widely publicized aims of these groups, Washington Police Chief Wilson gave the order early Monday morning, May 3, to abandon normal field-arrest procedures. The police proceeded to arrest large numbers of people, the number of arrests exceeding 7,000 on Monday (the greatest number of arrests in a single day in the history of the United States) and over 12,000 by Wednesday.

A large number of people protested that they had been arrested illegally, some indicating that they were just walking down the street on their way to work when they were arrested. In fact, less than 100 people were actually convicted. The procedures used by the D.C. police prompted American Civil Liberties Union Executive Director, Aryeh Neier, to charge that they constituted preventive detention, since detention for trial, as the number of convictions attests, was impossible.

The mass arrests have stimulated much controversy. Some critics have suggested that the great majority—people going to work, students coming out of restaurants, curious bystanders, and peaceful dissenters—were arrested on the unconstitutional grounds of guilt by association with a small handful who were doing violent acts, such as slashing automobile tires and in other ways destroying property. Others have argued that the police abandonment of normal arrest procedures violated another constitutional guarantee, the need for probable cause before one can be arrested. They point to the arrest of over 12,000 and the conviction of less than 100. As Senator Edward Kennedy (D.) of Massachusetts stated, "thousands were 'detained' on the basis of no evidence at all. Others were called for trial and came to trial where there was not the slightest basis for trying them."

On the other hand, the actions by the Washington, D.C., police were praised in many quarters. Supporters of police procedures argued that public authorities had a responsibility to keep the bridges and streets open and a responsibility to achieve this with a minimum use of force. The large numbers of protesters further added to the difficulty of the situation, for by abandoning normal arrest procedures, more police were released from "paperwork" duties and were available for greater periods of time on the street. During a discussion of the May Day procedures before a Senate Committee hearing, Richard Kleindienst, then President Nixon's nominee for Attorney General, stated:

> If I had to do it over again, taking into account the conditions and the circumstances that existed on Monday morning, May 3, I would have hoped that everybody involved in it in the discharge of their responsibilities would have done what they did. And knowing the potentiality for the consequences that could have occurred out of that situation, I have often given a prayer of thanks and relief that it worked out as well as it did, from the standpoint of society generally, the maintenance of order here in our Nation's Capital, and the lack of injury to any of the participants.

He further argued that constitutional rights were "scrupulously defended and preserved," for due process occurs only after one is arrested, not before, and assures that one is able to post bond on bail and is then given a speedy trial.

The May Day arrests clearly bring into sharp focus the dilemma of a society faced with mass and possibly violent protest. Did the police act responsibly in this situation or did they act unconstitutionally? Do police officials have the right to arrest those who they fear *may* commit punishable acts or must they wait until the actual acts are committed?

Compiling Data Banks

Citizens in a New York suburb became indignant when they learned that their local police department was spying and maintaining dossiers on local residents. The individuals involved were not criminals, but ordinary citizens who had participated on occasion in peaceful dissent activities involving civil rights, Vietnam war protest, etc. One instance cited was a 1968 speech by Eldridge Cleaver during which the police recorded license-plate numbers of cars in the parking lot.

This was not an isolated incident. Other nearby New York communities and nearby states, such as New Jersey, maintained similar surveillance practices and data. Reports from major cities, including New York City and Chicago, showed large numbers of policemen secretly engaged in undercover work involving suspected subversives. In 1969, the Chicago *Daily News* reported:

> undercover police investigations in Illinois are at an all-time high. In the Chicago area alone, more than 1,000 men from FBI and various other federal, state, county and city agencies are working on supersecret assignments.

It was also discovered that the United States Army was involved in domestic surveillance activities during the late part of the 1960s. The collection of data by the army was not limited to militant extremists but included ordinary citizens and even prominent citizens. In fact, even members of Congress were not immune. When Senator Edmund Muskie of Maine, the 1968 vice-presidential nominee of the Democratic party, was being prominently mentioned as that party's 1972 presidential nominee, he was put under surveillance for his attendance at and participation in an "Earth Day" pro-environment rally.

Reports of such incidents resulted in cries of protest across the country and prompted Senator Sam Ervin to begin Senate Committee investigations on the extent of such surveillance, on what was done with the information, and on who had access to such information.

During the course of his investigations, Senator Ervin became aware of the scope of national "data banks," the computerized storage of surveillance and other information on private citizens. He found that the Civil Service Commission maintains a "security file" containing more than two million index cards and a "security investigations index" covering more than ten million personnel investigations conducted by government agencies since 1939. He also discovered that the Department of Housing and Urban Development maintains over 300,000 names of individuals or firms and that other agencies which keep data-bank files include the Department of the Army and other military departments, the Bureau of the Customs, the Department of Justice, the Department of Health, Education, and Welfare, the Census Bureau, and even the National Science Foundation.

Senator Ervin found the prospect of having a government maintain such an extensive array of data banks on thousands of its citizens, frequently without citizen knowledge or, more importantly, citizen access, was both dangerous and frightening. He has cautioned:

> The new technology has made it literally impossible for a man to start again in our society. It has removed the quality of mercy from our institutions by making it impossible to forget, to forgive, to understand, to tolerate. When it is used to intimidate and to inhibit the individual in his freedom of movement, associations, or expression of ideas within the law, the new technology provides the means for the worst sort of tyranny. . . .

Supporters of government surveillance and the maintenance of data banks rest their arguments upon the need of a society for security. The Kerner Commission recommended that police authorities become more informed about various individuals and events in order to prevent or deal with civil disorders more effectively. In fact, such information as obtained from government surveillance may have already helped to save both lives and property, but may have denied personal privacy as a result.

Speaking to the difficulty of distinguishing between those engaged in legitimate dissent and those engaged in illegal dissent, Senator Roman Hruska (R.) of Nebraska has argued that one must keep in mind the fact that often groups which begin as legitimate and peaceful may end as subversive or violent. Consequently the gathering of information on dissenting groups, a process as old as civilized government itself, can only serve the greater interests of the society. The "chilling effect" which Senator Ervin suggested is responsible for inhibiting the exercise of First Amendment freedoms may also be seen as being responsible for inhibiting the exercise of subversive or violent activities.

How much surveillance should a government be able to conduct in a free society? What types of controls, if any, should be placed on those who collect and store data and on those on whom the data is collected? Is the maintenance of data banks consistent with a free society?

National Security, Dissent, and Presidential Power

The question of how society should restrict dissent and protest received renewed relevance as a result of testimony given before the Senate Select Committee on Presidential Activities (i.e., the Senate Watergate Committee), which revealed a number of illegal and unethical activities engaged in by various officials to counteract dissent against government policies and leaders. In particular, Jeb Magruder, the former deputy director of the Committee for the Re-election of the President, admitted to approving burglary and taking other steps, including the committing of perjury, to prevent detection and punishment. Former Presidential advisor on domestic affairs, John Ehrlichman, discussing his role in the break-in of the office of Daniel Ellsberg's psychiatrist, testified that he believed the President of the United States was constitutionally justified in taking whatever steps he deemed necessary—legal or illegal—to quell dissent wherever such dissent threatened national security. Does a President of the United States, in the belief he is protecting national security, have the constitutional power to engage in both legal and illegal acts, even when such acts clearly violate individual rights and individual liberties?

The examples cited in this chapter suggest some of the ways that have been used in recent years to meet the challenge of dissent and protest. The choice of how to deal with dissent and protest presents Americans with a very real dilemma. As Senator Birch Bayh (D.) of Indiana has stated:

We have a delicate balance to keep in our society, to maintain a society that is both free and secure. And if we are not very careful, we could get over that line and have a very safe and secure society without our precious freedom.

Chapter 8

Alternative Futures

As we have seen, dissent and protest pose grave problems for a society. The character and extent of dissent and protest in a society as well as the methods that society uses to deal with dissent and protest tell a great deal about the nature of the society. Questions with respect to these subjects have been posed throughout this book. As you have dealt with these questions, you have undoubtedly made certain assumptions on which your decisions were based about the relationship of dissent and protest to a society. This chapter explores several of the assumptions underlying previous proposals suggested to deal with dissent and protest in an effort to bring those assumptions to their ultimate conclusions. Three types of societies are presented and said to exist in the year 2000 A.D. Each society is based upon different assumptions and thus each possesses different characteristics. Before proceeding to the year 2000, you may wish to take a few moments to state explicitly your assumptions about dissent and protest. As you read of these three societies, which one of them seems to share the same types of assumptions you profess? Is that the type of society in which you would prefer to live? If none of these societies reflects your assumptions, what type of society would reflect them?

Harbinger

When Mr. Stanley opened the door leading to the large room serving as the association's meeting place, Mike Phillips was confronted by what appeared to be a scene of sheer bedlam. People were swarming across the room, their voices

121

raised to almost unbearable decibel levels. Slogans were visible everywhere, blanketing the walls and appearing throughout the crowd on hand-held placards. Some people were sobbing, others were fighting, but most were engaged in vehement argument. Seeing Mike's shocked look of disbelief, Mr. Stanley interpreted the scene for him. "This is a plenary session of the association of Harbinger," he said. "It is a typical session. Don't be alarmed."

Mike Phillips had recently recovered from a severe case of cancer. The disease had been diagnosed back in 1975, when he was 22 years old. Unable to provide a cure at that time, his doctors had recommended cyrogenics, the process of freezing the body until a cure could be discovered and then bringing the body back to life. It was now the year 2000. While a cure for Mike's affliction had been discovered in 1996, the backlog of cases was such that he had not been treated until recently. In the 25 years since Mike's body had been frozen, many changes had taken place in society. Mike's problem was to understand these changes and adjust to them. Mr. Stanley had offered to help Mike in that process.

Continuing to explain the scene confronting Mike, Mr. Stanley indicated that Harbinger was an "association," an assemblage of people numbering approximately 400. "But there appear to be more than 400 people in this room," Mike noted. "In fact, I would say that there are almost twice as many people as that in this room." Mr. Stanley agreed with Mike, adding that population figures were somewhat deceiving for they were subject to wide fluctuation. "Sometimes," he said, "there are only about 250 people and at other times the number reaches 1,000. But 400 more closely approximates the general level of those associated with Harbinger."

Mike found it difficult to understand the term association. He was amazed to find that by the year 2000 associations had replaced what were formerly referred to as villages, towns, cities, and even states. Apparently none of these existed any more. "Associations," Mr. Stanley continued, "are voluntary gatherings of people joined together by common interests and purposes. They are subject to continual redefinition of purpose and character depending upon who has recently left or who has recently joined the association. Since membership is in a constant state of flux, frequent meetings or gatherings of association members are necessary to decide on matters affecting them. Why, I've known associations to change completely in character in the space of one week.

"Other forms of organization have been tried, forms you probably recall such as towns and cities, but each of these has been found wanting. Associations developed because of their tenuous character. You see, no formal rules govern their structure. There are no constitutions, no written laws. Associations are whatever their constituents want them to be. People stay as long as their needs are met. When they disagree with the policies of the association they leave and move to another association more to their liking."

"Amazing," Mike commented. "What a great idea! Life seems to have become much freer than the life I recall in the 1960s and 1970s."

"No question about that, Mike," replied Mr. Stanley. "You see, with the abandonment of all formal rules and regulations, concepts you are familiar with such as money, private property, marriage, family, armies, and even taxes have all vanished. There are no moral codes, no ethical codes to guide behavior. There's no such thing as right or wrong. People are completely free to do as they wish. One is able to seek out or establish an association to meet his particular needs."

Mike was fascinated by this new world he had entered. He continued to press Mr. Stanley for additional information, and he was very pleased to discover that Mr. Stanley was more than willing to supply such information. "Actually, Mike, the impetus for this whole movement toward associated life came from the 1960s and 1970s. History records those two decades as years of terrible strife—much violence, crime, hatred, and greed. The very fabric of society was challenged. Something had to be done. It was quite obvious that it was impossible to maintain a single, stable society. Too many groups wanted too many different types of life-styles implemented for a single form to be predominant. Thus, associations began to develop during those decades. Remember how communities restricted to only white or black or red or yellow or brown-skinned people existed? Remember the communities that restricted membership on the basis of one's religion? Do you recall the formation of the retirement communities which required a resident to be over a certain age—60 I think—or the various communes limited to those under 30? Well, that was the start, and from that start the idea just accelerated. It was the only sensible way to accommodate the diverse needs and interests of the people."

"Yes, I remember that," Mark replied. "I remember how various groups were engaged in protesting against restricted entry requirements, against the enforcement of conformity to standards of behavior, against the maintenance of certain institutional patterns, like schools and the army. In fact, I remember how within a few years it began to become unfashionable to be married, or if you were married, unfashionable to have more than two children. And I remember how it became the thing to do to avoid service in the army or to oppose compulsory school-attendance laws."

"Well, that process only continued to accelerate during the last half of the twentieth century," Mr. Stanley went on. "In fact, here in Harbinger there are no such things as formal marriages or formal families. Schooling is not required and did you know that we don't have an army or even a police force?"

"Have all the armies, and all the police forces disappeared?" asked Mike.

"No, they haven't," was the answer. "Other associations have them. In fact, some associations might be best described as military associations. They are very aggressive, attacking neighbors, taking over the land or the products that the other association had."

"But," puzzled Mike, "how is it possible to protect yourself without a police force or an army? Aren't you afraid of those other associations?"

Mr. Stanley shook his head and smiled. "We don't worry about that Mike. If someone wants the land we occupy, we move. If someone wants the food we have grown, we are willing to share it with him. There are more important things in life than the mere ownership of property."

"But," pressed Mike, "what if some people come to Harbinger and want to kill all of you or force you to work for them against your will?"

"But why would someone want to do that to us?" asked Mr. Stanley. "We have no quarrel with anyone. We will let others have what they feel they must have."

"Suppose that someone wanted to kill you just for the sheer enjoyment of it? What would you do then?"

Again Mr. Stanley smiled. "Obviously, Mike, you pose a difficult question, one I don't know if I am prepared to answer completely. If it came to that perhaps I would defend myself, but, since I will not carry weapons, what could I do? More than likely, however, I would leave Harbinger before the situation had deteriorated to that point."

The discussion continued for a few more minutes before Mr. Stanley indicated that he had other duties to attend to. After he left, Mike sat pondering what he had just been told. How very much society had changed. People were really free from external controls to do whatever they wanted. There were virtually no restrictions on them. How wonderful!

Yet as Mike thought about this he remembered other things Mr. Stanley had told him. There were no external controls to restrict people but there were no forces to protect them either. In other words, there was no guarantee that one would be really able to exercise or enjoy the freedom he thought he had. With no protection, what was to prevent one of the militaristic associations from seizing Harbinger's inhabitants and forcing them into a form of slave labor? What was to prevent other people from taking land Harbinger had cultivated, or crops Harbinger inhabitants had raised, or houses Harbinger inhabitants had built? And if other people could do that, what good would theoretical freedom be? In fact, was it really possible to enjoy that freedom? Or did that freedom only seem to exist, its realization denied to all but the physically strong? Can freedom really exist without any kind of restrictions? Was Harbinger the type of association in which Mike really wanted to live?

"We Are Ready To Vote.
Push the Proper Button To Register Your Position."

(Margaret Thomas, her husband Robert, and their 14-year-old son Bryan are sitting at the dinner table eating the evening meal exchanging information about the day's events.)

MARGARET: Connie Alberts stopped by today and dropped off her cartridge tape of "The Sound of Music." What a great old movie that is! I think I must have seen it eight times by now but I still enjoy it.

ROBERT: I do, too, even though technically it is a terrible movie. It's so corny, but I enjoy the corn. It brings to mind how as a young boy I went to see it at Radio City Music Hall in New York City during the Christmas season. Hmm . . . standing in a line stretching for blocks just waiting for the chance to go in and see that movie.

BRYAN: Are you kidding? Standing in a line blocks long just to see a movie? I'd never do that! Why didn't you get a copy of the movie and see it at home?

R: But that was when movies were not available in tape cartridges. If you wanted to see a movie, you had to go to a special place to see it. And Radio City Music Hall was a special place—a movie, dancing girls, comedians, an organ concert, and a pageant on the stage. It was great.

B: Sounds silly to me. I can't picture myself standing in line in the middle of winter for anything, much less to see a movie. I'll bet you were frozen.

R: Yes, son, I was very cold. I had to wait three hours in line to get inside. But I really enjoyed doing it.

B: Enjoyed it? Standing in line three hours in the winter just to see a movie. I'll never understand how you could enjoy that!

R: I guess not. It's hard to explain, especially when today there are no special movie theaters and you can buy a cartridge tape of any movie you wish to see and view it in the comfort of your own living room. But there's still something special about that experience at Radio City. It makes me wish movie theaters would come back into existence.

B: I don't think they will ever come back. They're as obsolete as the gasoline engine. I know I would never pay to go someplace to sit in the dark with a room full of strangers just to watch something I could see much more comfortably at home. Besides, weren't they voted out of existence in the 1980s?

M: Yes, they were. I think it was in 1982, in fact. I remember the great debate about whether we could afford the luxury of buildings used so infrequently for such frivolous purposes when the housing problem was so severe. It was a big issue that year. Uh . . . that reminds me. Isn't the immigration vote scheduled for tonight?

B: Yes, it is. And I've decided how I'm going to vote. I'm voting to stop all immigration. We have to.

R: Well, I disagree. I say we must continue to permit immigration. After all, the United States was founded as a home for the discontented, for the dispossessed, for those seeking new opportunities. It's our heritage. We can't close the doors.

B: But Dad, this is the year 2000. We can't afford to have any more people come to this country. Look how crowded we are now! There just isn't any more room.

M: Bryan's right. If we don't stop all immigration we must face the consequences. I'm afraid that the proposal by the

LRMLP [Limited Resources Means Limit People] group will then be accepted. I don't like the idea of permitting only one child for every two families. I want Bryan to be able to have a child of his own.

R: But it is not an "either-or" proposition. I too, oppose the LRMLP proposal. It's humankind's natural right to have children.

M: We can't have both worlds. If we don't bar immigration we must limit family size.

B: Mother's right, Dad. You must rid yourself of your old-fashioned thinking. You have to change with the times.

R: No, I don't. I support the APPAH [American Patriots for Perpetuating America's Heritage] proposal. And I know of a number of other people who agree with me.

M: Well, we will see tonight. The vote is to be taken shortly after nine o'clock.

(Further discussion continues. After the meal is over and the table is cleared, the members of the Thomas family attend to other affairs. At precisely 8:45, a loud clanging noise sounds. Each of the Thomases goes to the living room and picks up a small rectangular box with a small screen and a number of different colored buttons on it. Each pushes the green button which stops the clanging noise, and then each pushes the red button which switches the image from the small screen on each box to the large screen on the side wall. Within seconds, a neatly dressed woman appears on the screen.)

WOMAN: Good evening, fellow citizens. As you know, tonight we are to decide on one issue—whether we should continue to permit immigration to this country or whether we should discontinue immigration. Five spokespeople are with us tonight, each representing the views of at least 20 million citizens as determined in our recent primary survey. Each spokesperson will have five minutes to present one view, after which all citizens will vote.

Our first spokesperson is Marcia Donaldson, representing American Patriots for Perpetuating America's Heritage, or APPAH as it is commonly called. Ms. Donaldson.

(Each of the speakers presents an opinion on the issue. Following the presentations, the woman reappears.)

WOMAN: Thank you. Now, citizens, you have heard the various arguments on this issue. You have had time to read, discuss, and consider this issue. Soon we will vote to decide the government's position. As you know, in accordance with the amended Constitution of 1989, we are no longer a republic but are now a direct democracy. You vote on each issue before the government with majority vote determining the position of the government. Each vote is instantaneously recorded in Washington. The collective vote will appear on the screen and your individual vote is recorded on your personal data file here in Washington. Remember, it is your civic duty to vote. You may elect to neglect this duty only five times a year before you are subject to prosecution.

We are now ready to vote. If you wish to permit immigration to continue, you should press the yellow button on your EVC box. If you wish to stop all immigration, you should press the blue button. And if you wish to abstain on this issue, you should press the white button. Press the button of your choice now.

(The Thomases press the buttons of their choice on the EVC boxes they hold in their hands. On the side-wall screen, the woman has disappeared and in her place are three horizontal columns which reflect the total vote and the percentage total. The numbers are constantly changing. Ninety seconds later the numbers are fixed, signifying that all votes have been registered. The citizens of the United States have again decided by majority vote another issue before them.)

"Can't We Be Free and Secure?"

I must not think about it. I must think about something else. No . . . no, it's no use. I can't. I can't. I don't know when I've ever been so depressed. Everybody and everything seems against me. Even my body seems in conspiracy against me. My head throbs, my eyes sting, my stomach hurts, my feet are numb. I'm numb. . . .

My mind is racing. I'm searching in vain for an explanation. But none comes. I can't explain it. How could this have happened? Why am I here in jail? All I've ever wanted was to be a good husband and father and a good teacher. I never wanted to be famous or controversial. I'm not an evil man. I'm not a wild-eyed radical. I don't want to remake the world. All I want to do is to live a quiet, self-respecting life. But I can't. They won't let me. Why won't they let me? Why? . . .

How long have I been here? It seems like forever. How long has it been since I've seen Francie or the kids? An eternity? I miss them so terribly. I've hurt them so much. The abuse they have had to take on account of me. I can see how much they've been hurt. I can see their disappointment. They don't really understand. It's for them, not just me. I'm not in here just for me, just for some type of ego gratification. I'm doing it because it's the right thing to do. . . .

It is right that they must suffer for my actions? Am I really just being selfish? Is it really worth it? Shouldn't I just give in? Shouldn't I beg for mercy? I'd be home again, I'd be with my family. Yes, it would be all right again. We'd be together; we'd be happy again. Why stay here in this miserable place? Why be stubborn? Sure . . . why be stubborn? Guard . . . I'm going to call the guard. I want out, I want to go home. I don't belong here. I want to be home with my family. Guard, guard. Guard, come here. Sure, that's what I'll do. I'll call the guard; I'll tell him it's all been a big mistake. I must have been crazy. Sure, I'll be able to go home again. . . .

Home to what? Could I work? Who would hire me? Who would want to hire someone who has spent the last two years in jail, someone who has been branded an enemy of the government. A traitor. Yes, a traitor, that's what the judge said. But I'm not a traitor. I love my country. I'm doing this *for* my country. Why don't they understand that? Why doesn't Francie understand that? It's for her that I'm in here, it's for our children, it's for our government. It's for all of them. That's why I'm here. It's for all of them. I'm not the one who is wrong. No, I'm not wrong, the government is. . . .

Ha! Ha! Ha! I'm not wrong, the government is. That's a joke. Isn't that the line that all traitors are supposed to say? Don't they think they are in the right? Pomposity! How much more pompous can you be? "I'm not wrong, the government is." What a laugh!

But it's different. It's different, I tell you. It's freedom— that's what it is. It's freedom that I'm fighting for. That's why I'm here. This is supposed to be a free country. This is supposed to be a country in which diversity is valued. Doesn't freedom mean diversity? Without diversity can one be free?

Diversity is a strength of this country. Our strength has been to allow various points of view to be expressed, to choose from what some have called the "marketplace of ideas." What's happened to that tradition? Why isn't diversity valued anymore? How did we lose that tradition? Where did we go astray? We have lost it and with it we have lost our freedom. We're not free anymore. Why? What went wrong?

I remember very well being young during the late 1960s and most of the 1970s. They were turbulent decades, decades when too much diversity existed. Things were constantly being challenged, from the family unit to the very institutions themselves. Everything seemed to be held in question. That was too much. Now there's too little. Why?

We had to do something in those decades. Some feared the country would split apart, would destroy itself. But we didn't act irrationally. No, we didn't act blindly. We took considered steps to erase the *abuses* that existed. We needed security to enjoy freedom. No one can be free unless he is secure, can he?

I remember how many newspapers we once had. The city had eight at one time but something happened. Newspapers began to disappear. Hmm . . . there were only two left in the city by 1978. Now there is only one.

Remember the attack on television and radio which was launched in the 1970s? We had concluded that there was too much violence, too much sex, too much emphasis on crime and criminality on television and radio. There was, remember? We couldn't permit that, could we? We had to clean up television and radio, didn't we? We needed to emphasize the good rather than the bad. Too many people were becoming depressed, too many people were becoming convinced that this was an evil country. It isn't. We had to correct that false image. Remember severely curtailing revenues when stations refused to accept the guidelines established by the government? Remember taking stations away from those who refused to abide by the guidelines? These were rational steps. Television and radio had too much influence not to be checked. That was the right thing to do. We needed to do that. People had to see the good in life. . . .

Then the magazines. They started to fold almost unnoticeably at first. *Saturday Evening Post, Look, Life*—giants of their day. Too expensive to produce, too expensive to send by mail, little subscriber interest, inability to compete with television—those were the reasons given. And the others? Of course, the others. But we had to do that, didn't we? We had to rid ourselves of the pornographic ones that were flooding the country at the time. We had to stop that. And, of course, we had to get rid of the violent magazines, the radical political journals, and those that constantly carped at the government. They were contributing to a deteriorating society, a society plagued by mass outbreaks and mass demonstrations, a society with an unreasonably high crime rate. The very institutions of society were being threatened. We couldn't permit that to continue. We needed stability.

And the schools, we had to take steps there. From the university to the grammar school, radicals infested every level. We had to weed them out; we could no longer afford to have our children exposed to their influences. We had to stop that, didn't we? We couldn't afford to continue to finance individuals who were urging the destruction of the society. The oaths we established to insure loyalty, the personality tests we administered, the ending of tenure—all of these steps were necessary.

And the crime rate. It was staggering! We had to make people safe. They were afraid to walk the street at night. Few people felt safe. The government had to provide security. The government needed the right to wiretap to break up organized crime, to weed out domestic subversives, to find out who the criminals were, what they were planning to do. Undercover agents were a legitimate weapon, data banks were important devices to control their activities. The use of bugging devices was necessary to prevent crimes from happening. So was the use of preventive detention. And so, too, were the diagnostic tests to reveal early tendencies toward antisocial behavior. Wasn't it best to find that out early? Wasn't preventive justice better than justice after the fact? Weren't these steps necessary to provide a secure society?

And that controversial vote we took, wasn't that necessary, too? People were abusing the so-called "Bill of Rights" and most of us didn't really believe in it anyway. Pornography, violence, riots, all types of antisocial behavior were being fostered by things such as "freedom of speech, freedom of assembly," and so on. The hands of the authorities were so severely tied that the honest man was no longer safe in his home or on the street. We needed to protect him, not the criminal. Repeal was the only sensible thing to do.

Then things started to improve. The riots stopped, the street demonstrations diminished, the crime rate fell. Life became more simple. We were safe, we were secure, we didn't have to battle with obnoxious people or obnoxious ideas.

But here I am in jail. I'm a good person, why am I here? I'm a teacher. All I did was to try to lead my students to truth. I only suggested that the Vietnam war was not a popular war, that the government may have erred in some of their decisions in the conduct of that war. After all, the textbooks didn't bring that point out. They glossed over that part of the war. But you need to know that, don't you? We can't hide that, can we? You need to know of the agonizing the country went through concerning the Vietnam war, otherwise you miss the whole point of it. Students need to know the truth about Vietnam. That's what education is all about, isn't it?

That's all I did! I only tried to bring out that point. But no one agreed with me. Even the university professors who testified at my trial disagreed with me. They argued that knowledge of citizen discontent during the Vietnam war was not essential, certainly not essential for high-school youth even if such discontent did exist. They argued, in fact, that to suggest such a thing was to foster discontent with the present government, was to stir things up, was to corrupt young minds. But that's not what I set out to do! I was just pointing out the truth. I . . . oh, what's the use?

No one seems to care. That's the worst of it. No one seems to care at all. I'm all alone in this. Guilty of one of the most basic crimes of humankind—the crime of heresy. We may be a secure society, but we are not a free society. Do we have to be one or the other? Must we be either free or secure? Can't we be both?

Chapter 9

Activities and Resources

Social Action Activities

The following represent several activities in the area of dissent and protest. They are presented as suggestions for translating one's feelings and thoughts into social actions.

1. Use the following form entitled "Methods of Expressing Dissent: An Attitude Survey" in conjunction with two basic questions: (1) How willing am I to use this method of dissent?; and (2) How effective is this method of dissent? Using a one-to-five scale, indicate your responses to these questions. [Note: 1 = least willing or least effective; 5 = most willing or most effective.]

Methods of Expressing Dissent: An Attitude Survey

Method	Rating
1. Attend public meeting to express views	1 2 3 4 5
2. Write letters to public officials	1 2 3 4 5
3. Vote for different public officials	1 2 3 4 5
4. Campaign for and/or contribute to political candidate	1 2 3 4 5
5. Sign or circulate a petition	1 2 3 4 5
6. Physically threaten those representing different views	1 2 3 4 5
7. Join or form an organization sharing similar views	1 2 3 4 5
8. Picket in front of the offices of public officials	1 2 3 4 5
9. Picket in front of the homes of public officials	1 2 3 4 5
10. Write a letter to a local or regional paper	1 2 3 4 5
11. Buy space in a local paper to present your views	1 2 3 4 5
12. Beat up those who represent different views	1 2 3 4 5
13. Organize or attend a public rally	1 2 3 4 5
14. Participate in a public march through your community	1 2 3 4 5
15. Publicly disobey a valid law to publicize your dissent	1 2 3 4 5
16. Publicly disobey what you consider an invalid law	1 2 3 4 5
17. Destroy public or private property	1 2 3 4 5
18. Shout down those with whom you disagree	1 2 3 4 5
19. Assassinate public officials	1 2 3 4 5
20. Engage in a boycott or strike	1 2 3 4 5

Administer this attitude survey to other groups and compare their responses with yours. For example, you may wish to administer this survey to other members of your class, to the members of other classes, to the faculty of your school, or to the parents of the members of your class. For comparison purposes, tabulate an average "score" for each item and then rank the items in order from lowest score to highest score. How do you interpret your findings?

2.   Visit the office of a local or regional newspaper and ask to go through the newspaper "morgue" (i.e., files of past issues). Find those incidents which occurred locally that could be classified as examples of types of dissent. Clarify and categorize them over a period of time such as a year, three years, five years, etc. What conclusions can you reach about the nature of dissent and protest in your local community (e.g., subjects of dissent, type of participants, tactics employed, success of such efforts, etc.)?

3.   Survey the literature on dissent in the school library and/or the community library. You may wish to ask the librarian questions such as the following:

(a) How extensive is literature dealing with dissent (e.g., what percentage of the total volumes in the library deal with this topic)?

(b) What is the nature of the periodicals—are many points of view represented or just a few? Are radical (far-left) and reactionary (far-right) views present?

(c) Does any group exist which must approve books before their purchase? In school libraries do students, faculty, administration, and librarians all have an opportunity to recommend books of their choice and have them purchased?

(d) What policies exist with respect to the books that are purchased? Who makes those policies?

Based on your findings, what opportunities do you feel exist for individuals in your community to read dissident literature? How do you explain your findings?

4.   Survey the textbooks used in various school courses, particularly in social science and language arts. How often is dissent and protest mentioned? What types of dissent are included? How is dissent treated—objectively, sympathetically, or critically? Does the treatment of dissent differ within a subject area (e.g., between history courses and sociology courses)? Does the treatment of dissent differ between subject areas (e.g., between social-science and language-arts courses)? How do you explain your findings?

5. Attend a meeting of a local protest group to become more familiar with its goals and methods. Invite a representative to visit the school. Perhaps you may wish to establish a current-affairs-type program featuring the representatives of various groups on a regular basis. Include groups representing a variety of points of view (e.g., John Birch Society, Young Americans for Freedom, Black Panthers, Americans for Democratic Action, etc.).

6. Use the following form entitled "Dissent and Protest Policies: A Community Survey" to uncover regulations that exist with respect to the expression of dissent and protest in your

Dissent and Protest Policies: a Community Survey
Regulations on Dissent and Protest in _____
(name of community)

Type of Activity	Time Limitations	Available Areas	Permit Required?	Special Conditions Necessary
Marches and/or parades				
Circulate and distribute leaflets or pamphlets				
Meetings in private homes or private buildings				
Meetings in public buildings				
Holding of mass rally				
Circulation of petitions				
Forming an organization				
Picketing				
Use of loudspeaking equipment				
Inviting a controversial person to speak in the community				
Speaking on public streets or in public parks				
Removal of public officials				

community. Use this survey to ascertain regulations on dissent and protest in the public schools. Compare community policies with school policies. How do you explain your findings?

7. If you feel that dissent and protest activities with respect to a certain issue are unjustified, you may wish to become involved in that agency, institution, individual, or policy which is being subjected to criticism. What opportunities are available to

counteract dissidents? Become active in activities designed to support your ideas.

Selected Resource Materials

The following represent items selected from among the diverse types of materials available on the subject of dissent and protest. Included are books, articles, movies, filmstrips, records, tape recordings, and even Congressional hearings, all of which are suggestive of the various ways in which one might approach the subject of dissent and protest. The scope of the suggested materials exceeds that of this book in the hope that they may be used to supplement its contents. Items were selected on the basis of their relevancy to the subject, their overall quality, and their convenience of access. Categorization is not exclusionary. Hence, one interested in the topic of black dissent may find appropriate materials under (1) "Anatomy of Black Protest"; (2) "The Ethics of Dissent"; and (3) "Is Contemporary Dissent Justified?".

1. Anatomy of Black Protest

Ambur, Neil. "Black Power in Sports: From Protest to Political Perspective," *New York Times,* Section 5 (March 12, 1972), pp. 1–2. (Analyzes militancy among black athletes.)

Belfrage, Sally. *Freedom Summer.* New York: Viking Press, 1965. (A personal account.)

"Black Politics: New Way to Overcome," *Newsweek* (June 7, 1971), pp. 30–39. (Describes efforts of black legislators to use political power.)

Carmichael, Stokely, and Hamilton, Charles V. *Black Power: The Politics of Liberation in America.* Vintage edition. New York: Random House, 1967. (Highly recommended.)

Cruse, Harold. *Rebellion or Revolution?* New York: William Morrow, 1968. (Valuable analysis.)

Fishel, Leslie H., Jr., and Quarles, Benjamin. *The Negro American.* Glenview, Illinois: Scott, Foresman, 1967. (Valuable source book tracing history of blacks from Africa to the 1960s.)

Franklin, John Hope. *From Slavery to Freedom.* 3rd ed. New York: Knopf, 1967. (Authoritative history.)

Grier, William H., and Cobbs, Price M. *Black Rage.* New York: Basic Books, 1968. (Work by two psychologists.)

Hamilton, Charles V. "The Nationalist vs. the Integrationist," The *New York Times Magazine* (October 1, 1972), pp. 36–51. (Which direction for blacks?)

"I Have a Dream . . .": The Life of Dr. Martin Luther King, Jr. (35 min., B/W). Available for rental from BFA Educational Media. (Good overview of Dr. King and the black protest movement during the 1950s and 1960s.)

King: A Filmed Record . . .: Montgomery to Memphis (B/W). Available for rental from the Martin Luther King Foundation, Inc. (Excellent chronicle; highly recommended despite its length.)

King, Martin Luther, Jr. *Stride toward Freedom.* New York: Harper & Row, 1958. (Valuable account of the Montgomery bus boycott.)

————. *Why We Can't Wait.* New York: Harper & Row, 1963. (Includes rationale and "Letter from Birmingham Jail.")

Lomax, Louis. *The Negro Revolt.* Signet edition. New York: New American Library, 1962. (Recommended; a history of the growth and development of the movement.)

My Life With Martin Luther King, Jr. Records. Available from Educational Record Sales. (Narrated by Coretta King with excerpts from Dr. King's major speeches; 3-record set.)

Peck, James. *Freedom Ride.* New York: Simon and Schuster, 1962. (Firsthand account.)

Quarles, Benjamin. *The Negro in the Making of America,* rev. ed. London: Collier-Macmillan LTD., 1969. (Valuable short history.)

"Report from Black America," *Newsweek* (June 30, 1969), pp. 16–35. (Series of articles providing insight into the black mood of America in the late 1960s.)

Report of the National Advisory Commission on Civil Disorders. New York: Bantam Books, 1968. (Important commission report on the 1967 disorders; highly recommended.)

Urban America, Inc., and the Urban Coalition. *One Year Later.* Praeger, 1969. (An assessment of the nation's response to the Kerner Commission's report.)

We'll Never Turn Back (30 min., B/W). Available for rental from CCM Films. (Details the events of "Freedom Summer"; produced by SNCC.)

We Shall Overcome. Record. Available from Scholastic Audio-Visual. (Songs of the Sit-ins and Freedom rides.)

2. Anatomy of Student Protest

Altbach, Philip G., and Laufer, Robert S. "Students Protest," *The Annals of the American Academy of Political and Social Science*, vol. 395 (May 1971). (Excellent source; contains valuable articles and an excellent bibliography.)

Bander, Edward J. *Turmoil on Campus*. The Reference Shelf, vol. 42, no. 3. New York: H. W. Wilson, 1970. (Contains selected magazine and newspaper articles, particularly for the years of 1969 and 1970.)

"Class of '69: The Violent Years," *Newsweek* (June 23, 1969), pp. 68–73.

Crisis at Columbia: Report of the Fact-Finding Commission Appointed To Investigate the Disturbances at Columbia University in April and May, 1968. First Vintage ed. New York: Random House, 1968. (Highly recommended.)

"End of the 'Youth Revolt'?" *U.S. News and World Report* (August 9, 1971), pp. 26–31.

Foster, Julian, and Long, Durward (eds.) *Protest! Student Activism in America*. New York: William Morrow, 1970. (Excellent compendium; highly recommended.)

Harris, Louis, and Associates, Inc. *A Survey of the Attitudes of College Students*. Study No. 2030. June 1970. (Provides valuable insight into the attitudes on campus during the 1969–1970 academic year. Also valuable for familiarizing students with statistical data and questionnaires.)

Jacobs, Paul, and Landau, Saul. *The New Radicals: A Report with Documents*. New York: Random House, 1966.

Keniston, Kenneth. *The Uncommitted: Alienated Youth in American Society*. New York: Dell Publishing, 1960.

——. *Young Radicals: Notes on Committed Youth*. New York: Harcourt, Brace & World, 1968. (Two valuable works by a psychologist who has written widely on student activism.)

——. "You Have To Grow Up in Scarsdale To Know How Bad Things Really Are," *New York Times Magazine*. (April 27, 1969). (Highly recommended.)

Lipset, Seymour Martin, and Altbach, Philip G. *Students in Revolt*. Boston: Houghton Mifflin, 1969. (A survey of the international student revolt; useful perspective.)

Miller, Michael V., and Gilmore, Susan (eds.). *Revolution at Berkeley*. New York: Dial Press, 1965. (Valuable collection, includes Mario Savio's "An End to History.")

Westby, David L., and Braungart, Richard G. "Class and Politics in the Family Backgrounds of Student Political Activists," *American Sociological Review,* vol. 31 (October 1966), pp. 690–692. (Noteworthy analysis of activist backgrounds.)

3. Anatomy of Anti-War Protest

Ashmore, Harry S., and Baggs, William C. *Mission to Hanoi.* New York: Berkeley Publishing, 1968. (Detailed account of events during the Johnson years.)
All Quiet on the Western Front (105 min., B/W). 1930. Available for rental from Universal 16. (Excellent anti-war movie; book may be used if preferred.)
"Amnesty for the War Exiles?" *Newsweek* (January 17, 1972), pp. 17–26. (Good overview on a controversial aspect of protest; contains data from opinion surveys.)
Berrigan, Daniel. *The Trial of the Catonsville Nine.* Boston: Beacon Press, 1970. (Account of the trial; provides an important look at both the man and the incident.)
Duscha, Julius. "Should There Be Amnesty for the War Resister?" *New York Times Magazine* (December 24, 1972), p. 6ff.
The Green Berets (141 min., color). 1968. (Good example of a pro-war movie. Events involve Vietnam.)
Hiroshima and Nagasaki. Filmstrips and records. Available from Inquiry Audio-Visuals. (Commentary by Norman Cousins; explores the question of the use of nuclear weapons.)
Kahin, George McT., and Lewis, John W. *The United States in Vietnam.* New York: Dial Press, 1967. (Documented, thorough account of United States policy in the 1960s.)
Nuremberg. A simulation kit. Available from Interact. (Explores moral-legal dilemmas for an individual and a society.)
The Pentagon Papers. New York: Bantam Books, 1971. (The controversial account of the development of American policy based on various government documents and studies.)
Reston, James. "War Leaves Deep Mark on US," *New York Times* (January 24, 1973), pp. 1 and 17. (Highly recommended.)
Ripley, Anthony. " 'The Movement,' with the War Ebbing, Ponders Its Role in a Nation at Peace," *New York Times* (February 18, 1973), p. 66. (Recommended.)
Taylor, Telford. *Nuremberg and Vietnam: An American Tragedy.* New York: Bantam Books, 1970. (Explores question of whether Nuremberg applies to US policy in Vietnam.)

Trial at Nuremberg. (26 min., B/W). (History of Nuremberg with actual film clips.)

Vietnam: BFA/CBS Audio History Series. Tape Recordings. Available from BFA Educational Media. (History of US policy in Vietnam; includes growth of anti-war movement.)

4. The Ethics of Dissent

Antigone (88 min., B/W). 1962. With English subtitles. Available for rental from Audio-Brandon Films. (May use the play if preferred. Explores the question of the existence of a higher law.)

Bedau, Hugo Adam, ed. *Civil Disobedience.* New York: Western Publishing, 1969. (Good collection.)

Civil Disobedience (Filmstrip with records.) Available from Guidance Associates. (Highly recommended.)

Coffin, William Sloane, Jr. "Not Yet a Good Man," *New York Times* (June 19, 1973), p. 39. (Highly recommended.)

Fortas, Abe. *Concerning Dissent and Civil Disobedience.* New York: New American Library, 1968. (Highly recommended.)

"Genesis 2:4 to 3:24," *The Holy Bible.* (The classic condemnation of dissent; highly recommended.)

Ibsen, Henrik. *An Enemy of the People,* in Armstrong, Gregory (ed.). *Protest: Man against Society.* New York: Bantam Books, 1969, pp. 15–91.

King, Martin Luther, Jr. *Letter from Birmingham City Jail.* Philadelphia: American Friends Service Committee, 1963. (Classic; highly recommended.)

Lynd, Staughton, ed. *Nonviolence in America.* New York: Bobbs-Merrill, 1966. (Important collection including works by King, Muste, Thoreau, etc.)

"Matthew 10:1–42," *The Bible.* (The Christian ethic of Jesus.)

Nixon, Richard M. "Transcript of President's Speech to the Nation in Answer to Watergate Charges," *New York Times* (August 16, 1973), p. 24.

Revolution. Filmstrip and record. Available from Guidance Associates. (Comparative look at various revolutions and the question of violence.)

Rock, J. S. "The New Math: The Day They Bombed Wisconsin," *Ramparts,* vol. 1, no. 7 (February 1971), pp. 32–34. (Valuable insight on this incident and the presentation of a rationale for bombing; highly recommended.)

Sevareid, Eric. "Dissent or Destruction," *Look* (September 5, 1967), p. 21.

Vickers, George (ed.). *Dialogue on Violence.* New York: Bobbs-Merrill, 1968. (Important and useful collection of essays on the suitability of violence as a means of protest; highly recommended.)

"Violent Protest: A Debased Language," *Time* (May 18, 1970), p. 15.

Viorst, Milton. "Dr. Benjamin Spock—Meet the People's Party Candidate," *New York Times Magazine* (June 4, 1972), pp. 42–58. (The making of a dissenter.)

5. Is Contemporary Dissent Justified?

The Alienated Generation (Filmstrip and record.) Available from Guidance Associates. (3-part filmstrip set which explores the reasons for contemporary protest.)

The Bill of Rights in Action: De Facto Segregation (22 min., color). Available for rental from BFA Educational Media.

Birmingham, John, ed. *Our Time Is Now.* New York: Praeger, 1970. (Underground newspapers, etc.)

Black History: Lost, Stolen or Strayed? (58 min., color). 1969. Available for rental from Bailey Film Associates. (Highly recommended.)

Brown, Dee. *Bury My Heart at Wounded Knee.* New York: Holt, Rinehart & Winston, 1970. (History of the American West from an Indian perspective; recommended.)

Cohen, Mitchell and Hale, Dennis. *The New Student Left.* Boston: Beacon Press, 1966. (Excellent overview.)

Color Us Black (58 min., B/W). 1968. Available for rental from NET Film Service. (Overview of black militancy; identifies important themes.)

Deloria, Vine, Jr. *Custer Died for Your Sins.* New York: Macmillan, 1969. (Highly recommended.)

Fanon, Frantz. *The Wretched of the Earth.* New York: Grove Press, 1963. (Influential work on colonialism and the third world.)

Feuer, Lewis S. *The Conflict of Generations.* New York: Basic Books, 1969. (Fruedian analysis of student protest.)

Friedan, Betty. *The Feminine Mystique.* New York: Norton, 1963. (The book that helped to spark the contemporary feminist movement.)

The Hand (Animated movie, 19 min., color). 1965. Available for rental from Contemporary-McGraw-Hill Films. (Explores the relationship of the individual to society.)

Hayden, Tom. *Rebellion and Repression.* New York: World Publishing, 1969. (Contains testimony before Congressional committees.)

Hentoff, Nat. "Why Students Want Their Constitutional Rights," *Saturday Review* (May 22, 1971), pp. 60–63ff. (An important look at schools and the Bill of Rights.)

High School (75 min., B/W). 1969. Available for rental from Zipporah Films. (Produced by Frederick Wiseman; a classic dissent using the cinema verité technique.)

Hole, Judith, and Levine, Ellen. *Rebirth of Feminism.* New York: Quadrangle Books, 1971. (Recommended.)

Jencks, Christopher. "Busing—the Supreme Court Goes North," *New York Times Magazine* (November 19, 1972), p. 41ff.

Hook, Sidney. *Academic Freedom and Academic Anarchy.* New York: Coles Book Company, 1969. (An outspoken opponent of student activism of the 1960s.)

Kennan, George F. *Democracy and the Student Left.* Boston: Little, Brown, 1968. (Critical of student activists, book contains letter written in reaction to author's criticism.)

Keniston, Kenneth. *Youth and Dissent.* New York: Harcourt Brace Jovanovich, 1971. (Collection of some of his best articles.)

Messner, Gerald, ed. *Another View: To Be Black.* New York: Harcourt Brace Jovanovich, 1970. (Worthwhile.)

Morgan, Robin, ed. *Sisterhood Is Powerful: An Anthology of Writings from the Women's Liberation Movement.* Vintage edition. New York: Random House, 1970.

Portrait of a Minority: Spanish-Speaking Americans. Filmstrips and records. Available from Scott Educational Division. (Highlights the plight of Spanish-speaking Americans.)

Power of My Spirit: The American Indian. Filmstrips and records. Available from Inquiry Audio-Visuals. (Narrated by Buffy Sainte-Marie; features Indians of diverse backgrounds and ages discussing their thoughts and feelings.)

Reich, Charles A. *The Greening of America.* New York: Random House, 1970. (Popular work which discusses the impending cultural revolution pioneered by the young.)

Reische, Diana, ed. *Women and Society.* New York: H. W. Wilson, 1972. (A general overview of feminism.)

Roszak, Theodore. *The Making of a Counter-Culture.* New York: Doubleday, 1969. (Recommended.)

Rubin, Jerry. " 'What the Revolution Is All About,' or 'We Are All Vietcong and We Are Everywhere,' " in Armstrong, Gregory, ed. *Protest! Man against Society.* New York: Bantam Books, 1969., pp. 156–160.

Viva La Causa: The Migrant Labor Movement. Filmstrip and record. Available from Inquiry Audio-Visuals.

What Do You Kids Want Anyway? Filmstrip and record. Available from Inquiry Audio-Visuals. (Explores causes of dissent.)

Women: The Forgotten Majority. Filmstrip and record. Available from Inquiry Audio-Visuals. (Narrated by Gloria Steinem; examines causes of women's liberation movement.)

6. Society and Dissent

"The Biggest Bust," *Newsweek* (May 17, 1971), pp. 24–29. (An account of the May Day events in Washington.)

The Bill of Rights in Action: Equal Opportunity (22 min., color). Available for rental from BFA Educational Media. (Open-ended investigation of case in which a black is given preferential treatment as means of counteracting effects of racial discrimination.)

Cleghorn, Reese. "When Readers Become Suspect," *Current* (September 1970), pp. 42–46. (Details Treasury Department efforts to obtain names of people who have checked out certain books from public libraries.)

Federal Data Banks, Computers and the Bill of Rights. Hearings before the Subcommittee on Constitutional Rights of the Committee on the Judiciary, United States Senate, 92nd Congress. 1st Session. 1971. (Important look into the extent of government efforts to obtain knowledge on private citizens, particularly dissenting citizens.)

Federal Handling of Demonstrations. Hearings before the Subcommittee on Administrative Practice and Procedure of the Committee on the Judiciary. 91st Congress. 2nd Session. 1970. (Explores federal handling of dissent in Washington, D.C.; recommended.)

Methvin, Eugene H. "Where Does Liberty End and License Begin," *Reader's Digest* (May 1972), pp. 77–81.

Nominations of William H. Rehnquist and Lewis F. Powell, Jr. Hearings before the Committee on the Judiciary of the

United States Senate. 92nd Congress. 1st Session. 1971. (An opportunity to explore with various Senators the attitudes of two men who were ultimately confirmed as members of the United States Supreme Court.)

Rights in Conflict: The Walker Report to the National Commission on the Causes and Prevention of Violence. New York: Bantam Books, 1968. (Important work on the 1968 disturbances in Chicago.)

Skolnick, Jerome (Director). *The Politics of Protest: A Staff Report to the National Commission on the Causes and Prevention of Violence.* Washington, D.C.: United States Government Printing Office, 1969. (An important and valuable work; highly recommended.)

Organizations

The following is but a brief list of various national organizations active in the area of dissent and protest. The address given is that of the national headquarters.

American Civil Liberties Union, 156 Fifth Avenue, New York, New York 10010

American Friends Service Committee Incorporated, 160 North 15th Street, Philadelphia, Pennsylvania 19102

American Legion, 700 North Pennsylvania Street, Indianapolis, Indiana 46204

Americans for Democratic Action, 1424 16th Street, NW, Washington, D.C. 20036

Anti-Defamation League of the B'nai B'rith, 1640 Rhode Island Avenue, NW, Washington, D.C. 20036

Center for the Study of Democratic Institutions, 2056 Eucalyptus Hill Road, Santa Barbara, California 93103

Citizens for Clean Air, 502 Park Avenue, New York, New York 10022

Common Cause, 2100 M Street, Washington, D.C. 20037

Congress of Racial Equality (CORE), 200 West 135th Street, New York, New York 10030

Daughters of the American Revolution, 1776 D Street, NW, Washington D.C., 20006

Democratic National Committee, 2600 Virginia Avenue, NW, Washington, D.C. 20037

Friends of Earth, 30 East 42nd Street, New York, New York 10017